ABUNDANCE, THE ASPIRATION AND HOPE OF ALL MANKIND

HOW THE ABUNDANCE MINDSET CAN ENHANCE HUMAN CONNECTEDNESS, SOLIDARITY, ATTRACTION, EXPANSION AND THE ONENESS OF MANKIND.

TOMBUH DAVID LATEH

ISBN 979-888546889-3

This work is dedicated to all my children, daughter- in-law and grandchildren.Thank you for loving me, praying for me and wishing me well.

God bless you mightily.

TOMBUH DAVID LATEH

Contents

Purpose And Forward

Iam highly honored and exited to assemble these ideas in this piece of work because I feel indebted and obliged to explain and convince my readers that the concept of 'the mindset of abundance' is the source of all abundance. I am very enthusiastic about the expression 'abundance.' Of course, it is the aspiration and hope of all mankind.Having immersed myself deeply in the research on the concept of the mindset of abundance, I amhonored to encourage my readers to acquire this mindsetas they seek abundance in wealth, position, authority and influence. No individuals or society can maintain any sustainable abundance in the absence of themindset of abundance, even when in possession of great wealth, resources, influence, authority and potentials. Without the mindset of abundance what is available will be consumed greedily, jealously, stingily and for self-interest by the 'powerful' in society. Society will again be back in lack, scarcity and want. I have been moved by my love for the creation of an abundance society to put these ideas together for my readers. This book is very helpful to the entire reading public because the mindset of abundance must be the possession of all mankind but those who will make the greatest application of the book are adults in any field of human endeavor.

In this piece of work, the point is firmly established that abundance is the aspiration and hope all mankind. We can vividly recall to our minds that the human beinghas a built-in tendency to gravitate towards the environment, society or situation of profuseness or plenitude. This is natural behavior exhibited by all living things. Where there is ample supply, plenitude and great quantities of whatever that satisfies human need, human movement is in that direction. Wecan even put it in clearer terms by saying that there is always movement from an area of scarcity to that of abundance.

But what is abundance? Many conceive abundance in terms of plenitude, amplitude, profuseness or great quantities of any substance. This is quite right, but there is more to it than just this. Abundance is a concept that describes the mind. It's a concept of the mind. It is a mindset that is hopeful and believes that there is always enough to go round and satisfy all. The abundance mindset believes that our societies and the world in general are all packed full with substance, wealth, opportunities, natural resources, possibilities, potentials, capabilities, abilities, gifts and competencies for all mankind. All these constitute what may be called the wealth of the nation. These great resources make all our societies and the universe full of abundance. This is the creator's desire for all his creatures, you and me included.

Problems come in as a result of the scarcity and lack mindset. This mindset has trapped and gripped mankind in lack, scarcity, poverty and want. When we think lackor scarcity, there is no way we can come into abundance for what we think and concentrate on, is what we receive. If what occupies our minds is scarcity and lack, we are conditioned to see the resources in our society and the world as scarce, inadequate and unable to go round. Under this scarcity condition, we are therefore compelled to fight our way through to have what will keep us alive. This fight is demonstrated in hoarding, embezzling, corrupting,misappropriating, banking abroad and trying in our own ways to exclude others. And as we succeed in these evil plans, the resources arerendered scarce, inadequate and unable go round to all.

The scarcity mindset is a limiting mindset and is the source of all evil. It is characterized by a very high-level senseofhoarding, self-interest,jealousy, envy and the exercise of greed by those privileged to handle public funds. With this mentality our societies are unable to grow, change and produce abundance. So, we grapple with society and acquire wealth, power, position and influence with the hope to attain our satisfaction, fulfillment and happiness. Unaware that satisfaction, happiness and fulfillment do not come from the ownership of substance and wealth.We then set out for more wealth,position and influence with the hope that more can do. In this great spiral led by a deceitful hope, we end up asking ourselves is this all there is? Where is the satisfaction, happiness and fulfillment? Our hearts are still empty. Even if substance, position, power or` influence could produce abundance, our abundance would fluctuate with the fluctuation in the acquisition of these factors and we cannot call it abundance.Abundance does not fluctuate.

The abundance mindsetcaptures the understanding that there is always abundance in the universe. Therefore, abundance is a mindset. It is characterized by a positive mental outlook which is proactive, optimistic and expansive.It promotes solidarity, interdependence, cooperation and mutuality, human connectedness, the human spirit, sharing and caring. Without these values, it's difficult for any society to create abundance because what will stubbornly reign will be the giants'opportunity to always take the lion's share. When you think abundance and feel abundance, what is available is always enough. The mindset of abundance is a mindsetpregnant with the desire to share: encouragement, advice, correction, wealth, knowledge, information, development ideas, human and social concerns. This desire to share in the community makes everything available and abundant in our societies. Without themindset to share and care, which constitutes ahumanizing spirit, there can be no abundance for abundance is expressed in theability of humans to share, care, lift each other out of stressful situations and foster an inclusive spirit in the human family.

To create and nurture abundance, we must give up limitingbeliefs, values and the lack mindset, for we cannot rise above our beliefs and values. We must also reinvent ourselves by sharpening our skills and competencies in order to be useful to our society in producing abundance. The human being is totally his mindset. We are what we believe we are, and can do only what we believe we can. We can reach the sky or be failures, depending on what we think we can. Guard your mind and develop it to serve you. The abundance mindset is a growth mindset. It is expansive, proactive, hardworking and promotes solidary, cooperation and mutuality, sharing, fellowship and connectedness. It is a mindset of provision and should be the possession of all mankind.

Appreciation

I heartily extend my sincere and warm thanks to my mentors whose works I read and prepared myself for this piece of work. Thanks, immensely for mentoring me. I could not have done it without you. I thank you from the bottom of my heart. Your contribution to this work is really immense.

TOMBUH DAVID LATEH MSC. AGRIC. DEV.
JIKIJEM OKU BUI DIVISION
NW REGION OF CAMEROON
TEL: 699905364
EMAIL: davidlateh@yahoo.com

About The Book

Is this all to the life set before me? Where is the happiness, satisfaction and fulfillment? These and more are the usual questions posed by most people who have made amazing strides in the success of their plans, goals and dreams. To their greatest dismay, their hearts still lack happiness, satisfaction and fulfillment that supposedly accompany success. They are unaware that these values don't come from success in substance-wealth, power, position or influence. They flow from the mindset of abundance. Even if we were to go for the second and up to the tenth round,acquiring success in substance, we will still end up with hearts that are empty and the spiral could continue.

The abundance mindset is the source of our joy, happiness, satisfaction and fulfillment. It is cultivated by saturating our minds with thoughts of abundance-what you think and believe in your heart, is what you get. It is maintained by discarding the limiting believes of lack and scarcity. It is a proactive, positive mental attitude that is optimistic.It's underpinned by the humanizing spirit of the win- win attitude, solidarity, human interdependence, cooperation and mutuality. Its absence is possibly the course of dissatisfaction and stress which probably may lead to suicide or suicidal attempts. This may be possible despite the success in our dreams of wealth, position and power. This piece of work elaborates so much on these issues. Read it.

CHAPTER ONE

INTRODUCTION

This introduction to the chapters puts in summary form the topics treated in each chapter.It all begins from chapter 1 which deals with introduction to all chapters.

Chapter 2 gives us an understanding of what abundance is all about. The glimpse that we have here about abundance is that it is a mindset that is positive,hopeful and believes that there is always enough to go round.

Chapter 3 presents the characteristics of abundance, bringing to our understanding that the abundance mindset is positive, proactive and encourages solidarity, cooperation, mutuality and interdependence. This mindset is accompanied by humanizing values.

Chapter 4 presents the life of abundance as life lived in happiness, satisfaction and fulfillment,independent of substance, wealth, power, position or influence. Of themselves;substance, power, position and influence cannot generate our happiness, satisfaction and fulfillment.

Chapter 5 answers the question, is abundance a curse or a blessing? Abundance is a blessing not a curse. What obtains in resource-rich, developing countries is not actually a paradox as we are made to believe. Countries that are very rich in natural resources have poor development records. Reason being that these countries have been greatly exploited and looted by the rich developed countries and thereby retarding their development. In reference to these exploited poor countries, it would appear thatabundance is a curse.

Chapter 6 presents the law of attraction. The point here is that if you can develop your skills and competencies, refine your character, relationships and your health, so that you become attractive, you will attractopportunities.Great opportunities and possibilities will move towards you.

Chapter 7 deals with creating and nurturing abundance. The point is made that an abundance society should not be mistaken for an unambitious or complacent society. An abundance society must contain men with an abundance mindset who work hard to produce the inner and outer abundanceand make their society to move forward and advance making abundance available to all.

Chapter 8 presents the mindset of abundance. Man is altogether his mindset. The mindset of abundance is positive, hopeful, expansive, enduring, resilient and inclusive.

Chapter 9 presents the significance of the mindset of abundance, indicating that people with this mindset are happy, satisfied, fulfilled, relaxed and hardworking. They influence and impacttheir society with optimism and enthusiasm and with their skills and competencies.

Chapter 10 answers the question if abundance produces happiness, satisfaction and fulfillment. Since these values are cognitive qualities describing the state of our mindset, we simply can assign or call on the mind to produce these qualities as need be. This can be done with or without abundance in our society.

Chapter 11 presents authentic development as having the ability to produce an abundance society. Authentic development begins in the mind. It is characterized by the mindset that brims with the human spirit, solidarity, connectedness, human onenessand social advancement. These values coupled with an abundance mindset, can produce an abundance society.

Chapter 12 presents abundance as the aspiration of all mankind. Those who have the values of authentic development and are endowed with the mindset of abundance enjoy their society to the fullest. Their society is characterized by: interdependence, happiness, satisfaction, connectedness, peace, security and services. This is why a society of abundance is the aspiration and hope of all mankind.

Chapter 13 presents the purpose and end of abundance. The purpose of abundance is to make our societies embrace and enjoy mutual benefits, human solidarity,the ability to share, careand promote interdependence. The mindset of abundance can transform our societies.

Chapter 14 presents abundance in the future. Changes in the world of business, technology and economics will transform societies across the globe for the better. Mankind has to make the plans for this future abundance today.

CHAPTER TWO

WHAT IS ABUNDANCE?

This question comesup frequentlyand from many quarters. Those concerned are filled with the desire to understand this term, abundance. What is abundance?What does it really represent in the minds of those who know and use the expression often? Before now, I felt quite confident that I could answer the questions with relative ease. But in my attempt, I was awakened to the truth of this elusive concept.I thought in my mind that abundance is plenitude, profuseness, amplitude, bountifulness or immeasurable quantities.This is true, but there is more to it than just this. It could be that you also think in the same direction with me. If you do, then, to our amazement, the above answer is only part, not even the most significant part of abundance.

For better understanding, we may question further. Abundance of what? Abundance for who?Abundance for what? The answers to these questions unfold as one explores this text. Abundance is understood in many different perspectives.I have come to grips with the understanding that many conceive abundance not only in terms of plenitude or profuseness but in terms of who you are, how you think, perceive and manage your inner self.In thisperspective, substance-money, wealth and property are only part of abundance, not the main issue.This class of people in their conceptionof abundance attach a lot of weight to the type of mindset onemay carry along if oneaspires to enjoy abundance.The explanation being that you cannot have a mindset of 'lack' and at the same time aspire to achieve and enjoy abundance. It is a contradiction in terms.

A 'lack' mindset presents you to yourself and the world as poor and needy or living in scarcity. Yap May Ling, [p.39] makes the point that if most of your thoughts are of scarcity, envy, illness, or sadness, you will attract more of that into your life. So, attract abundance [wealth, health, joy, prosperity] into your life simply by learning how to harness the power of your thoughts.

A very acceptable situation is that you can carry along an abundance mindset but without substance. Under this condition, your mindset will present you to yourself and the world as a man of abundance that enjoyssubstance, full of wealth and prosperous. Substance or position may not be the highest attainable objectives in life. Those with great substance still wonder if this is all to the life set before them. In this life, we must take our time to think keenly and decide with wisdom. Why?Because there is the possibility to battle up to the top of the ladder of success in life at a great sacrifice, only to be made aware that the ladder leans on the wrong wall. This is why those with substance have no guarantee that they will enjoy happiness, satisfaction and fulfillment as well.

Many have stepped on others' heads, stolen the goods of society or used dishonest means to climb to the helm of power, position and influence in their communities. These individualswallow in remorse, regrets and unfulfilled lives despite their fantastic wealth, high positions, power and influence. They yearn for happiness, satisfaction and fulfillment to no avail.This remorse and dissatisfaction may probably lead to stress and possibly to suicide or suicidal attempts, notwithstanding their wealth, power and position. These wealthy people cannot enjoy the innerqualities of happiness, satisfaction and fulfillment. Why? Because thesequalitiesare solely the product of hearts soaked in conscience, solidarity, caring and empathy.But these wealthy and dishonest people have a deficit of these inner values. No doubt, there are those who have earned their substance, wealth, positions and influence by their honesty, dedication and hard work. For those lackin satisfaction, happiness, joy and fulfillment, they must add to their achiements the humanizing qualities of sharing, caring, solidarity, cooperation and mutuality. Without these qualities, our achievements will have a deficit that blocks our fulfillment and satisfaction.

Abundance is a property of the mindset that is hopeful and believes that there is always enough to go round. The abundance mindset believes that in every situation, everybody who is around and ready to share from what is on the table will enjoy enough."We are included in what is on the table andit will be enough for all of us," they say.They believe that our society always has enough of what it takes keep us comfortable. Thatthe world at all times is full of opportunities for all of us.

But those with the mindset of 'lack' will always hoard and capture for themselves what should be enough to satisfy everybody. In that case the distribution of what is available is skewed. This is the source of our lack, want, scarcity and suffering. Under these conditions there are 'haves' and 'have nots.' In this perspective, abundance is pictured as substance [prosperity and wealth] and is the possession of lucky or strong men and women in society. Those with this kind of abundance according to this concept, live sumptuously, affluently and greedily. They think and live their lives to themselves. The important question here is, do they have satisfaction, happiness and fulfillment as well? Certainly no.

An abundance mindset is such a marvelous blessing andgift thatit would appear that only fortunate people possess it. When you reflect in terms of abundance, you come to grips with the fact that the human, physical and spiritual environmentsare fertile with it. Abundance is always available. It exists even in great quantities. But most of the time we simply are greedy and self-centered. If we are called upon to give to our neighbors what we have, we would simply excuse ourselves that we have nothing. But what about the cheerful smiles on our faces; the hearty and warm greetings;the warm good morningexpression; the sincere- thank you; the God bless you; the have a good day; the warm welcome; the loving kiss; hug or embrace; the sweet goodbye and the loving connections?' If these expressions come from the heart, they cheer, warm and uplift. They encourage and spur our neighbors, colleagues, friends and others that cross our path.

These expressions are very satisfying as they lighten our burdens, sweeten our hearts and make us look and feel significant. Such encounters makethe day seemingly brighter and more beautiful, as sweet smiles loosen our faces. These expressions cost us nothing much, except that they take our time and attention. We can always give these freely, as we have received them freely. Theysweeten hearts and minds and make them gland. This indeed, changes the atmosphere of our societies.

There is always great abundancethat we can share with others but for reasons we cannot explain, the capacity to share lacks in our communities.In addition to the above blessings that God has deposited in us, he has also supplied our environment with free air, oxygen, wind, sunshine, rainfall, seas, seasons, fauna and flora, plains, valleys, deserts and hills. These truly constitute an abundant environment.Those with the abundance mindset reflect on these things with lots of appreciation and gratitude.Except for the air, wind, sunshine, seasons, oxygen and rainfall that are beyond our control, individuals and nations grab and control the others, using them greedily and stingily. This brings poverty, scarcity, lack, and want. If we cannot first share what comes from the heart, we hardly can share what is in our hand. Jeff Foster, in deeper meaning of abundance,[p 2] makes the point that abundance is not about getting what you want, it is not about filling a lack, it is about realizing that the present moment never lacks anything. It's already full to the brim with sights, sounds, smell, thoughts and feelings, colors and shapes, beyond imagination.

The abundance mindset has captured the understanding that there is always abundance in the universe including opportunities, human potentials, human connectedness, human concern in the physical, economic, spiritual, social, political and the cultural environment. In all these areas of human connection, there is abundance for everyone. But the spirit of human greediness, self-interest and self-centeredness encourage a few people to capture all and hoard for themselves. This is the cause of anxiety, scarcity, struggle and generally underdevelopment. Thank God that abundant life does not come from substance or material things. The life of abundance flows from our inner being. When we have opportunity to share knowledge, skills, information, advice and encouragement and when we fail to do so, we have failed to expand abundance, may be because of our greed, stinginess, jealousy and hatred. Or it could be because of ignorance on our part.

If abundant life were to come from possessions and positions, it would fluctuate as possessions and positions fluctuate. Abundance doesn't fluctuate for it is the goal of society. That would be very far from our true conception of the life of abundance. Derek O' Neill, in "what is abundance really?" [p. 1], maintains that abundance is a way of thinking and living even when you have less money, love or support than you would like. Life delivers a continuous set of circumstances. Living in abundance can give you a constant source of stability that is not based on external things, but you must change your perspective and believe in all the potentials that lie within your reach. Abundance is a state of mind. It can't be lost, taken from or bestowed on you. It is about what brings you joy and fulfillment, not about what you have.

Many others have embraced the mindset that urges them to look away from the enticing prosperity and wealth of the world. The typeof wealth that enslaves the human spirit and makes man a servant, not a master. They have also lovingly embraced the notion that abundance and the spirit of gratitude and appreciation should be recalled to human hearts. They have the feeling that to embrace this spirit of abundance is to open up space for greater abundance. The spirit of abundance can only inhabit those hearts that are filled to the brim with gratitude, appreciation and connectedness. Abundance is a personal as well as a social concept because the joy and fulfillment of the individual can also be extended to the social system.

Man must not be lured and driven by the spirit of possession, position, power, prestige and wealth. These things are important but not a necessity for our lives and living. Sometimes our focus is highly placed on them to the exclusion of more humanizing factors like solidarity, the win-win spirit, human connectedness, cooperation and mutuality and the oneness of mankind. Without these and more, we will certainly lack the human spirit that should exude from the social environment. We must constantly remind the human family about this humanizing spirit that should permeate and animate the human heart and our societies.

As important as wealth, property and position are to humanity, they remain important but not a necessity. Those whose lives are not absorbed by these values seem to enjoy more and are more satisfied and fulfilled. But then, there is nothing more important in life thanjoy, happiness, satisfaction and fulfillment. Abundance is manifested in the hearts of joy, satisfaction, gratitude and fulfillment. Leanne, in "is abundance about undeserved blessing?" [p.1] points out that it is time to look into our own hearts to see if we are showing gratitude for having more than we need. We need to look away from what the world tells us we should be piling up and then focus on being grateful for the abundance we already have and share some of that with those who have less than us. We can share our time, knowledge, talent and love-the things we have plenty of already and can afford to give away.

Believing in abundance is believing in more and more is a positive concept, therefore abundance is the possession of humans with positive mindsets. It is pregnant with hope, determination, a persistent and consistent spirit. Human beings who are filled to overflowing with the mindset of abundance, believe that whatever human, social, economic, cultural, spiritual and political resources available for our people will always be enough to go round. God in His creation of man, equipped and empowered him adequately with inner resources for his life on earth. In addition, He placed man in an environment of a rich variety of resources. Man, inwardly is therefore abundant in potentials, capabilities, abilities, skills and competencies. Outwardly, man is placed in an environment of great abundance-the forests, animals, seas and sea animals, wind, air, sunshine, minerals and fresh water supplies.

It is this mindset of abundance that arousesin man, the spirit of research, enterprise, innovation, experimentation, exploration, sculpture and others. Under this condition, the horizons of abundant life [thehuman, natural, capital and other resources that fulfill human need] are extended every passing day. Man's life is therefore lifted higher and higher every passing day. There are more promises of the abundant life as man visits the skies, moon, other planets and below theearth and sea bottom. As Tamara Carleton, in ''a measure of abundance,'' [p.1] points out, what holds constant is simply the believe in more. As a belief, abundance drives our faith and intentions around growth- at home, in business and in politics. We believe that more is a good thing and that achieving more in life is important for our personal satisfaction and to our national identity.

The positive mindset or the mindset of abundance makes a fertile ground for generosity, a welcoming spirit and human connectedness. This is because generosity and abundance are concepts hinged on the heart. The generous heart considers others first, before self. It is therefore not jealous, greedy, stingy or full of hatred. It is love and concern [qualities of the heart] that nurture the feeling that what is available can go round or reach out to everyone. The abundance mindset is a positive and outgoing mindset. It is an inclusive mindsetthatleaves no one out or behind. This makes abundance universal.

The 'lack mindset' is exclusive, limiting, egoistic, selfish and self-promoting. When the lack mindset is expressed, it is never that what is available cannot go round.In effect, such a mind has been captured by greed, the hoarding, embezzlement and manipulative spirit.Under this condition, what ought to be abundant, becomes inadequate. The reason for its inadequacy is that when the leaders 'that-be'would have grabbed the'lion's share,' the leftovers will not be able to go round. Scarcity therefore is not existing on its own but created by the "powerful" in society. The lack mindset is therefore characterized by self-centeredness, self-interest, self-aggrandizement, the win-lose spirit and the 'I,' 'my' and 'mine' syndrome.

The abundance mindset is endowed with powers and the ability to create and nurture the win-win spirit, solidarity, human concern, human oneness,fellowship and the sharing spirit in our society.Together, these form what is called the humanizing spirit. These values are warm, welcoming, encouraging and reassuring. This is the spirit that the American Founders planted in their offsprings. Martin Luther King makes an allusion to it in his great philosophy of abundance [p 3] he believes that America is a land of plenty with more than enough wealth for everyone and welcoming strangers is far less dangerous than closing the borders, minds and hearts.

Abundance can also be expressed in every level of our living. The human being is a social being. He receives fulfillment in so many aspects of his life in order to have a good measure of contentment. Remez Sasson, in what is abundance, definition and explanation, [p. 3] gets deep into the heart of the matter as he maintains that abundance is found in love, friendship, opportunities, food, good deeds, energy, trees, grass, matter, time and spirituality in life. We can picture that opportunity is found everywhere, in everything, natural, social or cultural. The abundance mindset is therefore what the creator has bestowed in all his creatures and wants them to become, have and be. If we reject this mindset it's because our hearts have become filthy, greedy and intensely self-seeking.

But when humans live in poverty and lack for long, they become trapped in it. This trapping is characterized by the spirit of accumulation,grabbing, self-interest, write your name on everything and claim, greediness and an expression of permanent lack. These characteristics constitute the breeding ground for embezzlement, mismanagement, misappropriation of public funds either in cultural and social organizations or in government. This is why most of our public funds cannot go round. They are in the hands of managersandpeople whohave a background history of being trapped and scourged by poverty for long. When appointed to positions of responsibility, they are excited and go mad. Their first concern is themselves not the public they are assigned to serve. They grab and stockpile public funds in their private accounts as if to prepare for eternal life on earth.

What remains true is that there is a great abundance in the universe. God endowed the human being with potentials, capabilities, gifts and opportunities. This reveals the benevolence and great concern of the creator for humanity. As if that was not enough, He then blessed the human environment with a rich supply of natural resources for man's enjoyment. All that mankind needs to do is to cultivate the awareness of God's abundance, available to all and for all. The mindset that is aware of God's abundance is a necessity to all mankind. Why? Because the mindset of lack, scarcity and poverty have brought all the underdevelopment and suffering on mankind.

We need to cultivate the spirit of human connectedness and the oneness of mankind. We may be people of different nations, tribes and ethnic groups but the blood that flows through our veins is the same. Our differences are so insignificant compared to our similarities. This spirit of the oneness of mankind should spur us to fellowship, enjoy the warmth of each other and develop the sharing spirit. In this way, we can enjoy God's abundance made available to all mankind. In this way also, the greed, tribalism, nepotism and our differences will disappear and we will become one, in fellowship, able to share in the abundance of God's creation, as onehuman family.

To Live in abundance means to live our lives together. Jeff foster, puts it better in the deeper meaning of abundance [p1] he maintains that abundance is not what you have but what you are. It is not the money you have in your bank account, the trophies on your shelf, the letters after your name, the list of goals reached, the number of people you know, your perfect body or your adorning fans. It is your connection to each breath.........It is your open heart, how deeply moved you are by love every day, your willingness to embrace and to hold what needs to be held.........

Abundance is quite an elusive concept because often, it has been thought of only in terms of wealth, property, money and substance. Life is lived in many dimensions and wealth or substance is just one. This is why most people have sacrificed much in the pursuit of wealth and substance, making their lives poor in many important areas. Often, we have sacrificed our priorities for substance. Money or substanceis important and make things easy for us but this might mislead us into thinking that life is all about money or money is all of life. Life is not made up solely of the things we possess. If it were so, the rich will live and poor will suffer and die. Thank God, it isn't so.

Substance and wealth should not blind our minds to the facts of friendship and human connectedness, human dignity, integrity and respect for all mankind, good deeds, concern for humanity, cooperation and mutuality.Life is lived together to enjoy the warmth that comes from fellowship. We are reminded in 'exercise to go from scarcity to abundance mindset' [p.1] that our abundance mindset is what brings us true joy and happiness from inside. While our cultures tell us to focus on material things that we lack, this is not the path of true abundance, even though having money makes life easier, it doesn't mean you will be happy: becoming obsessive about making more money can rob you of your joy now. Therefore, the aim is to pursue your dreams and grow while being happy and content with what you have now.

CHAPTER THREE

THE CHARACTERISTICS OF ABUNDANCE

The life of abundance is concerned with our desire to live our possibilities.The abundance mindset isthe human spirit that leaves no stone unturned in motivating us to take action and make things happen in our lives and communities.The life of abundance is a lifestyle that acceptshuman shortcomings and makes corrections.Thishelps us to learn and continue the journey, rather than blame ourselves or accuse others. It is lifelived with great concern for the welfare of others. A life of service, motivated by the win-win spirit. It is positive mindset that is concerned with possibilities. It nurtures and promotesour abundance. It is a mindset of expansion, growth, progress and multiplication.

The mindset of abundance is a great assert in human advancement. It is known for its ability to fire and inspire us to move on, even in the face difficulties. It urges mankind to move forward and upward and to explore the unknown world. The abundance mindset is therefore characterized by the desire to be more, produce more, enjoy more andaspire for more.Not just for self but for the purpose to create more forhumanity and society-increasing the wealth of nations,our stock of abundance.This is opposed to the scarcity mindset which produces for self and selfish reasons.

Because of their dissatisfaction with the status quo, those with abundance mindset are anxious to share knowledge, encourage learning and expansion. It isby this means that they bring opportunities and possibilities to all, leaving no one behind.All these, with the purpose to bring change and development to their society. The "five traits of an abundant mindset," [p 2] maintains that people with an abundance mindset focus on possibilities and what is working. They view failure as an opportunity to grow and learn about themselves and the world. They are masters. They focus on the long-term and are committed to everything they do. Most importantly, they are humble. They believe that to share knowledge, provide value and support others' growth, is important in living a life of service.

The abundance mindset is characterized by a positive mental outlook. It is hopeful, determined, enthusiastic and believes that success is the birth right of all. It encourages society to dream big, plan, set goals and objectives in other to achieve. The abundance mindset is proactive and encourages society to do what is possible and helpful. It encourages individuals and society to takedecisions that move them and their society forward and upward. It sees the best, hopes for the best and determines to do the best to create abundance for itssociety. Its leading characteristic is the win-win approach to life. The decision or resolution that is arrived at in a society of abundance is mutually beneficial to all because it considers all the parties with respect and fairness. Such a decision is therefore the best for all of them and is greeted with joy by all. The abundance mindset creates an environment in which everyone benefits and is satisfy. It is a universal approach to life. It creates a society of tranquility.

The mindset of abundance is one of optimism and planning,with hopes that things will begin and end well.It trusts and hopesthat more and more will be available for human happiness, satisfaction and fulfillment. The 'five traits of an abundance mindset,"[p.3] maintains that if you want to achieve anything in life, you need to maintain an optimistic belief that your desire will be satisfied. An optimistic and positive attitude is a precursor of a life of happiness, fulfillment and gratitude. Optimism means toapproach problems with a sense of confidence and high personal ability. Specifically,optimistic people believe that negative events are temporary, limited in scope, manageable and will soon be over. Everything can be taken from a man but one thing-to choose one's attitude in any given set of circumstances, to choose one's own way.

People with abundance mindset are absorbed in thinking good about others. They have a feeling and concern to assist and make life easy and comfortable for others. They believe in their hearts that what is on the table to be shared will go round and be enough for all. They never think lack, but abundance. They are confident that whoever is available benefits from the decision that is made and enjoys being part and parcel of the whole.

People with the abundance mindset have abundance flowing in their veins, words and hands. They are outgoing, like to give, serve, teach and learn. There is abundance in their thoughts and in their actions, which is extended to their neighbors and society. Wherever they are, their desire is always to leave a mark and particularly in the improvement of the quality of life in their society. Their goal is always to maketheir community better than they met it. Their thoughts, plans and the manifestation of abundance rub off on others. Bobby Albert, in ''3 traits that reflect an abundance mindset,'' [p 4] makes the point that abundance thinkers live lives of gratitude for the abundance of the world in which they live. They are positive and upbeat. To them, life is continually a replenished bowl of fruit-all ripe for the taking. They teach others how to be positive and livein gratitude.

It must be acknowledged with all gratitude that God is the supplier of all abundance. There is nothing that is, that was not made by Him. The Holy Scriptures say He made the heavens and the earth and everything therein. He is therefore the creator, supplier and maker of all mankind. He is the giver of joy, peace, love, grace, life, happiness, fulfillment and satisfaction. The creator placed these values in our inner selves. These are the highest values of the human society. These qualities are not found in substance,but dwell richly within us. When God fills our inner being with these qualities, he then provides the wealth, substance, property and other material resources to supplement our lives. Therefore, our sense of abundance doesn't comefrom material resources but from the inner self and then supplemented by material resources. Great emphasis must therefore be laid here, that in an abundance society, inner resources are supplemented by outer resources or physical resources. Under this condition there is great abundance of happiness, satisfaction and fulfillment in human hearts and minds.

Since human abundance is a combination of inner and outer resources, no one can be poor or rich just because of the absence or presence ofany of theseresources.Material resourcesconstitute just one aspect of human abundance. God put the inner resources in all mankind and no one lacks them. But in reality, our abundance comes from the inner self.Running after material resources and orchestrating all the jealousy, greed and hatred can never create the human abundance that satisfies our hearts. Material things alone cannot bring us happiness, satisfaction and fulfillment because the inner values are supposed to bring satisfaction to our hearts and lives, independentof material things.We are supposed to have inner joy, happiness, satisfaction and fulfillment even without material substance.

In no way do I down play on the importance of material things, but as important as they are, they have their place in the scheme of things. Jim, in ''10 characteristics of abundant life,'' [p.4] maintains that it's natural to worry a little because life happens and there are important things that concern us from time to time. But when we follow Jesus, we never have to get swamped with these concerns, nor should they ever become so overwhelming that stress and anxiety take us down. We give our stress and anxiety to him and continue in abundant life.

The abundance mindset believes that to make strides in our life- journey,we must dream big dreams, plant great plans in our heartsso that we can make our society a place to be. It is the mindset of abundance that holds that the horizons of wisdom, knowledge and achievements are constantly receding, thereby increasing abundance for mankind. The limitations placed against human achievements are constantly being overcome.New inroads are created that lead to innovations, new communication technologies, science, experimentation, exploration and enterprise. These are pathways that open to the creation of human abundanceand service to mankind. Human nature is that of constantly exploring new and meaningful opportunities that will unleash greater potentials for mankind. The abundance mindset is proactive, searches for ways to spur growth and make things work.It eases life and builds a society of abundance through theurge to teach, share, encourage and uplift. Torsten Caspa, in "discover the key traits of abundance mindset," [p.2] maintains that to "think big, opens horizons, lifts limitations from my life and enables me to achieve higher goals."

People with abundance mindsets are very mindful of their company. They are aware of the fact that those who accompany, share and interact with them, either build or dismantle their plans. They are either dreamers like them, dream thieves or dream killers. They must choose their company wisely, with the knowledge that they cannot be different than their company. Their company should be such as to make positive contributions to their lives and help themachieve their dreams. The people who surround them and take part in their discussions and other connections must bepeople that move towards their direction. People who also have a mindset of abundance-positive and optimistic. People who are prepared to advance and support the advancement of others. The "five traits of an abundance mindset,"[p.3] maintains that your vibe attracts your tribe. Your environment has a powerful effect on your behavior. If you want to live an abundant life, it is important that you surround yourself with people who ascribe to the same philosophy of thinking as you do.

CHAPTER FOUR

LIVING THE LIFE OF ABUNDANCE

We live in a world that is littered with advertisement platforms. These advertisements seemingly impress upon us the notion that man hasn't come near to what gives contentment and fulfillment in life. We are constantly being bombarded with information on the need to live in a more modern house; dress beautifully; own the latest car in town; command power; enjoy a high-level position and be looked up to and respectedor be counted among the Millionaires or Billionaires. This, we are told, is the source of joy, contentment, happiness, satisfaction and fulfillment. This certainly, is an illusion of the first order.We can quote many who possess these amenities and more,who still wonder and ask how they can obtain happiness, satisfaction and contentment.

If we could get our satisfaction, happiness and fulfillment from these sources, its implication would be that the billions of people in our world who will never access these amenities and resources will never dream of happiness, satisfaction and fulfillment. Moreover,if we aspire to secure our satisfaction and fulfillment from these things,we must be reminded that our joy will oscillate between failure and success,lack and abundance, for positions and possessions are never permanent in life. Satisfaction, fulfillment and happiness are permanent goals in life and cannot be staked on things that are temporary.

These people with substance and positions still wonder whether this is all to the life they have got to live. Their hearts are still empty and they are yearning for contentment and satisfaction despite their positions as billionaires or millionaires. In the mist of this confusion,they turn their eyes and minds constantly in the direction towards more wealth, more power, more position and more influence. When in possession of 'more,' their yearning hearts are still empty and this search for more continues.This is the great dilemma of human life. This is because we failed somewhere along our life's journey to convince the human heart that the abundance mindset is the source of our joy and fulfillment. The life of abundance is therefore very independent of wealth, power and position. Ruth Soukup, in living well and spending less [P.44] maintains that....... true contentment will never be found by looking outward. If we struggle with wanting the things, we see around us, we need to stop looking.

The life of abundance is lived independently of what we possess in terms of substance,or social status. We must be clear in our minds of what is important for us. It is clearly understood that wealth, property, position and power have not measured up to our contentment, satisfaction and happiness. Despite owning these things, our hearts arestill left empty, unfulfilled and we yearn for more. This is certainly a reminder to us that satisfaction and contentment are lodged in our inner selves. These values are not found in material things but in our hearts. Living the life of abundance, Ruth Soukup, in living well and spending less, [p.33] maintains that it is living a life rich in faith, family, friends and creativity. It is a life full of the richness that God has to offer, a life spent in building treasures in heaven rather than on earth. It is not a life of laziness and greed, but one of discipline, hard work and self-reflection.

To live the life of abundance meansthat we make connections that nurture and promote the humanity and integrity of mankind. It is to live our lives together.We must open up to all in our society and make everyone feel included, welcome and appreciated. Our lives must be engulfed in servicesthat maintainthe oneness and brotherhood of mankind. Our lives must be characterized by our quest to share, correct, forgive and aburning desire for the warmth of other members of society. Abundance is found in all of us.We multiply, share and enjoy it, only as we interact lovingly and peaceably with fellow human beings. After all, we are social beings wired to live our lives in communities. Such communities should have the anxiety toshare, commune, fellowship and encourage each other. They mustmaketheir contributions to move their society forward and upward.

This is the mission of humanity-to be our brother's keeper and to make the world a better place to be born, live and die. Jonatan Fields, ''in how to live the good life,'' [.19] maintains that life is about our contribution to the world, even if that world is a single person, in a way that is meaningful, in a way that matters and allows you to feel like you matter. It is to knowdeeply that you are doing the thing you are here to do.........It is to like who you are and accessyour full potential, your strengths and gifts, the deepest part of your humanity and leave nothing unrealized or untapped. You are fully expressed, seen and heard.

To live and enjoy the life of abundance or the good life, our love for humanity must be the leading factor. We must love fellow humans; show affection and intimacy for we cannot expect love without giving love. Whatever you do to others, you do it to yourself because our actions sometimes boomerang on us. The attitude to cultivate in living a life of abundance is to be a friend of all. Keep up your love, welcome and attract people with yoursmile.Laugh, play and enjoy the company of all, out of your love for humanity. Indeed, we should never dare to forget that all human beings belong to one great family, God's family. Under the aforementioned conditions, you would be making a wonderful contribution to a life of abundance in your society or community. This is the good life; you enjoy it and you contribute to it.

As a fellow citizen, while you have your expectation of people and society, your love and concern for the people must overwhelm. A community that lives in abundance must be characterized by fellowship, acceptance, sharing, belonging and allegiance. This is how to multiply our abundance. We put smiles and laughter on the faces of our people and live in oneness. Jonathan Fields, in "living a good life," [p.18] maintains that we are innately social beast, born to be with others. When we are with the right people in the right place, in the right way, magic happens. We come alive and our world, our capacity to flourish and grow and engage with life and enjoy, expands. When you are with the wrong people, in the wrong way, or isolated from the right people, everything shrinks.

Abundant life is life lived in Jesus because he himself is life and has promised abundant life to those who follow him. Those who follow Jesus enjoy abundant love, peace, happiness, success, satisfaction and fulfillment. All abundance and fullness dwell in him because he is our creator, sustainer, supplier and indeed, giver of all good gifts. The devil comes to steal, kill and destroy but Jesus comes to provide life in great abundance. He feeds our spirits and supplies our physical needs. As a follower of Jesus, you are called upon to enjoy Christ's abundance and not fall into the trap of defining your values in terms of substance-your wealth, position, power and what you have. Your value is determined and defined in terms of whose you are.You belong to the creator of the universe. Ruth Soukup, in living well and spending less, [p.41] quotes the book of Galatians 5:22, which maintains that the fruit of the spirit is love, joy, peace, patience, kindness, goodness, faithfulness, gentleness, self-control, against such there is no law.

God's abundance is lavished on his children and we can see this everywhere as revealed by the abundant air, wind, water, vegetation, fertile land, sunlight, underground resources, sea and land animals. The valleys, hills, plains and mountains all display God's supply of abundance to mankind. His aim is that his children should wallow in great abundance, for his name's sake, for he himself is abundance. His creation displays his magnificence and superfluity. The Lord is the God of abundance, giving generously to his children. When we fail to give him the first place in our lives, we are in a sense replacing him with substance, power, position and influence.

When substance occupies the place of God in our hearts, our hearts are never satisfied. They are empty or filled with the desire for more and more things, power and position. This provesthe inability of substance or wealth to give us the satisfaction we need. This quest for more will never end until we give God the place he deserves and desires in our hearts. When God the creator is acknowledged and given the first position in our hearts, our hearts, coupled with our entire being, will respond in superabundance. This is the source of happiness, joy, peace, satisfaction, success and fulfillment. Thisbrings contentment and joy to our hearts and our entire life.

Abundance must be received in the spirit of gratitude, love and gratefulness. For this is the spirit that should inhabit the children of the 'Most High.' Abundance is a precious gift from God and gratitude should be our response. To Live in gratitude to God is to live in acknowledgement that he is the supplier of abundance and giver of all good gifts. To Live in abundance calls for our gratefulness, thankfulness and appreciation. It meansto be connectedwith God and mankind. It's abundantly clear that when we show gratitude and appreciation for God's kindness, our abundance continues to flow,which makesus enjoy a continuous and unending flow of the good life.

To live in abundance is a precious gift from God and those who have put Him 'first place' in their lives have opened the channel to the flow of the good life. God is the God of all and the great provider for all. We only need to acknowledge Him as our father. As a father, he pours his abundance on us. In the same manner, just as an earthly father provides for his children indiscriminately, God provides for us. We only need to show our gratitude and appreciation. Jivita Jay, in "5 basic principles to attract abundance and prosperity in life," [p. 5[maintains that we need not want to be searching for big things to be grateful, we can start with simple yet powerful things. Every day we inhale and exhale without paying any attention to it even though our entire existence depends on our breath. So, we give gratitude for the breath we take. Give gratitude for the bright sunshine and the air we experience daily, not realizing their importance.

CHAPTER FIVE

IS ABUNDANCE A BLESSING OR CURSE?

A paradoxical relationship exists between the 'haves' and the 'have nots.' This paradox is a great prove that true abundance is a gift from God. In human terms, it is expected that countries of the world endowed with superfluous natural resources are well placed to advance faster than those lacking in these resources. Paradoxically, what we find in reality is the reverse. How come that countries richly supplied with natural resources should wallow in poverty, discrimination, conflict, undemocratic institutions, human rights abuses, inequalities and dictatorships? Countries with scanty natural resources have developed remarkably, leaving those plentifully supplied with natural resources behind. This is the paradox of development which has left mankind wondering whether natural resources are a blessing or a curse. What then is the value of natural resources to a country if they bring but curses instead of advancing the development process?

We cannot doubt this outcome after the experience of the looting during the periods of imperialism, colonialism and neocolonialism. These countries continue to be lowered down to their knees. This should be the logical outcome, that countries blessed with abundant natural resources should be cursed to look like deserts. The colonialists are all responsible for this resource- cursethat hangs on developing countries. So many theories, principles and paradigms may be advanced to explain the paradox of poverty in the mist of abundant natural resources. But surely, no one doubts that the colonialists have looted and carted away these resources for their advancement at the detriment of these countries.

The theories are propounded just to exonerate the developed countries from this looting and also to derail the development processin developing countries. Even the developed countries cannot doubt that they are responsible. It is even a paradox that the theorists refuse to see the looting and looters. They prefer to go on to propound theories to solve the resource-curse phenomena without pointing an accursing finger at the looters. What are theories for, when we know the causes and the effects? Why not get to the roots and lay bare the problem so it is starved to death?

The paradox of curse in the mist of abundance should not be made to look like a mystery for no one doubts that theseare the machinations of the developed countries. They loot through illegal exploitation themselves orsupportthe illegal exploitationof these resources for their benefit. Patrick Alley, in natural resources abundance, [p.3] maintains that the problems that face the logging industry include corruption, illegal logging and conflict. In 1996, the world bank estimated that Colombia could earn 100million dollars a year in their timber sector; Global Witness said it wasn't possible. In hindsight only 93million dollars was made between 1994 and 2000; less in 6 years accrued to the state and the country than what was projected as a single year's earning. During that time illegal exports were vast, [187million dollars in one year].

The resource curse is also known as the paradox of plenty. It embarrasses the world to imagine that people who have been favored by God's hand, to have in abundance what others need for their development, should have but curses and wallow in poverty and want. Some of these natural resources that may be the exclusive preserve of some countries include: timber, iron ore, gold, fossil fuels, diamond and other minerals. All these resources are in very high demand and are expected to bring in abundant foreign exchange.They are expected to build the roads and make development to spill over to other sectors of the economy. In this way, they will multiply and usher in our abundance. This makes life easy and comfortable for all citizens. But in reality, the reverse is true-abundant natural resources have nurtured but poverty, lack, inequality, autocratic rule, conflict and poor human rights records. All these and more result from the machinations of the developed countries in their dealings with developing countries.

All the machinations of the colonialists are calculated to create confusion in other to loot and cart away these resources for their own development. Wikipedia in resource curse, [p. 1] makes the point that the resource curse also known as the paradox of plenty refers to the fact that countries with an abundance of natural resources [fossil fuels and certain minerals] tend to have less economic growth, less democracy and /or worse development outcomes than countries with fewer natural resources. There are many theories and much academic debates about the reasons for and the exception to these adverse outcomes. Most experts believe that the resource curse is not universal or inevitable but affects certain types of countries or regions under certain conditions.

This paradox of plenty isonly about some countries in the developing worldwhich are considered resource-rich countries. These countries are blessed with great natural resources to harness for the development and multiplication of their abundance. Over the years, since the unset of imperialism and colonialism and contraryto human expectations, theseresource-rich countries are unable to feed, clothe and house their citizens, let alone create abundance for everyone.These countries are the properties of some developed countries called colonial masters. These poor conditions were initiated during their contacts with these colonial masters. They are most of the time in conflict, disputes, confusion, poor relations, disagreements, unrest, dictatorships, poor human rights records and generally characterized by threats.

These miserable situationsare fertile looting conditions created by these colonial masters. For in most cases, we find the colonialists at the background to incite the citizens to create confusion. Because it is in confusion that these evil agreements are forced on the governments of these countries. In their pretense to settle these disputes and conflicts, they negotiate very unrewarding dealsto cart away with these natural resources for their own development. Their eyes are always watching and monitoring the affairs in resource-rich countries expecting conflict, wars and confusion to visit these countriesat any moment. They either jump in to exploit by carting away the resources or by selling their guns for the perpetuation of the wars.

The resource-poor countries do not receive the same attention as there are no resources to loot in those countries. This set of countries isvery privileged to be left alone and so they develop on their own and even faster. Wikipedia, in resource curse, [p.2] maintains that the International Monetary Fund [IMF] classifies 51 countries as resource-rich. These are countries that derive at least 20% of export or 20% of fiscal revenue from nonrenewable natural resources. 29 of these countries are low- and lower-middle income. Common characteristics of these 29 countries include [1] extreme dependence on resource wealth for fiscal revenues [2] low savings rate [3] poor growth performance [4] highly volatile resource revenues.

Under this condition, what isthe option for resource-rich countries? The best option is not to throw away these resources but to diversify into other areas of industrialization. This is an important option to consider if these cursed countries must free themselves from the curse of stagnation and underdevelopment. These countries must industrialize and develop other sectorsto make good use of whatever foreign exchange received from the natural resources. They must also monitor and let the law take its course on those carrying out the illegal exploitation of their resources.

These natural resource industries must spillover to other sectors of the economy like infrastructure, business, education, health and other productive sectors. In this way the economy will expand and increase employment opportunities. This is quite an important way forward for these set of countries. Erwin H Bulte, in "resource abundance, poverty and development," 2004 [p.3] makes the point that if natural resources are an inescapable curse, this may imply that countries endowed with natural resources can only develop by turning their backs on their comparative advantage and diversifying into other non-resource-based activities.

Is it really true, that fossil fuels, goldmines, our crop and wood plantations are unable to assist our countries in the generation of abundance for our citizens and to lift us out of the poverty trap?It is not really true that these resources are a curse, but that even the scanty proceeds from the resources and the resources themselves are indeed open to misappropriation.What is true also, is that when compared to industrial products, foreign exchange from these natural resources is open to misappropriation, corruption and bribery. These evils are rife in developing countries endowedwith these natural resources. Without leaders that are honest, transparent, faithful and accountable, it will be difficult for change to take place in these set of countries endowed with this natural wealth.

The proceeds from our plantations, fossil fuels, diamond mines, ores and wood should be able to spillover and generate industrialization, education, health, physical infrastructure and business, bringing abundance to our people. Erwin H. Bulte, in ''resource abundance, poverty and development,'' [p.3] the point is made very clearly that.........productivity gains in Agriculture and forestry have fueled high-tech innovations with both forward and backward linkages to other sectors of the economy [example, the Green Revolution]. Thus, natural resource-based activities can have high productivity, growth, technical spillovers and linkages to other sectors of the economy. The other question that remains unanswered is why some countries have harnessed these benefits and used resource rents judiciously while others have not.

If we consider the looting, bribery, corruption and misappropriation, we canunderstand that so much underdevelopment is being done. Action must therefore be taken to stamp out this evil activity to ensure that the population is lifted out of poverty to enjoy abundance. We cannot just accept and wallow in this resource curse. The government and the international community must rise up against this evil so that the people are liberated from poverty, inequality, dictatorship, human rights abuses, social exclusion and inhuman conditions. Under these hard conditions the people have resorted to conflicts, protests and being difficult to govern.

Measures must be instituted that safeguard our forest from illegal logging, ensure accountability, transparency and good management. No country can develop without democratic institutions, accountability, transparency, trust and good management-all ensuring good governance. Patrick Alley, in ''natural resource abundance; obstacles to development or harnessing resources for development,'' [p.4] makes the point that....... perhaps a coalition of governments should be formed to think of something new and imaginative. Legislation to ban the importation of illegally extracted logging is needed in the same way as other commodities are handled today. A definition is needed at the UN to deal with it quickly.......

A more solid way to solve this problem is to invest in human capital. Without investing in the people by developing their technical skills, potentials, capabilities, abilities, competencies and knowledge, the spillover or diversification from the natural resource industries to industrialization, infrastructure, business, education and health will not happen. Development is first of all concerned with people's minds. They must be given skills and competencies that make them productive in their fields of endeavors for you cannot expect from the labor force what you have not put into them.

When the people are prepared technically, emotionally and with competence, diversification will be possible as other sectors will begin to emerge and grow. When all the sectors have emerged and are booming, abundance will be made available to all. Old story, 'in risks are real,' points out that Norway always had her natural resources. It was only with the advent of the educated labor force that it became possible for Norwegians to harness these resources on a significant scale. Human capital accumulation was the primary force behind the economic transformation of Norway. Natural capital was secondary. The problem is not the existence of natural wealth as such but rather the failure to avert the dangers that accompany the gifts of nature.......

Most of the corruption, mismanagement and embezzlement Creep in to the natural resource industries because the situation is never clearly defined. The leaders that handle these resources see just much money in their hands and they begin to chip quantities of it for themselves. It is important and necessary that government defines in clear terms what quantities of the proceeds from the natural resources shall be ploughed back, the quantities for consumption, for education, health and investment in other areas of the economy. In this case money will not lie idle, opened for embezzlement. This work can only be effectively carried out by a good government with good institutions. Old story, in 'the risks are real,' maintains that for us to consider Norway, from day one, Norway's oil and gas reserves were defined by the law as common property reserves, clearly establishing the legal rights of the

Norwegian people to the resource rents. On this legal basis the government has absorbed about 80% of the resource rents over the years. God laid down economic as well as ethical principles [commands] to guide the use and exploitation of the oil and gas for the benefit of current and future generations of Norway.

CHAPTER SIX

THE LAW OF ATTRACTION

''What you think about, talk about, believe stronglyand feel intensely about, you will bring it about,'' says Jackcanfield. Thinking is a creative activity. By our thinking we form things and bring them into reality. We become what we think all the time. The law of attraction is the principle by which things come into our possession. We are imbued with the force of attraction that pulls things to ourselves and makes them ours. The creator of the universe made this law the possession or birthright of all mankind but very few are aware of, let alone use it for their benefit. This force is neither mysterious nor magical. Any human can learn and use this force.

One of the perspectives by which this law operates is learning for self-improvement or preparing ourselves to be alert in order to capture the opportunities and possibilities that cross our path in life. Success staff, in ''11 ways to attract abundance in your life,'' [p.3] maintains that opportunities and success are not things you go after necessarily, but things you attract by becoming an attractive person. If you can develop your skills, keep refining all the parts of your character, yourself, your health, your relationship, so that you become an attractive person, you will also attract opportunities. Opportunities will probably seek you out.

Also, the law of attraction is a principle of giving, for giving generates abundance. To beopen, to share or give outsubstance or ideas and information to people is amarvelous way to attract abundance. The mystery is that what we give out, grows, multiplies and comes back to us in great quantities. Therefore, an important way to grow in abundance and be a blessing to others is to give generously. It is in giving that we receive our abundance, for without giving, there is nothing to multiply. God the creator, has blessed us greatly with substance, ideas, wisdom, intelligence, love, joy, peace, opportunities, capabilities and potentials. These blessings come to us and members of our community so that we can share together and be a blessing to each other. In this way, we make this abundance available to all in the society. Therefore, we ought to be generous with these blessings by giving freely to others and to our community. Just as freely as we receive, let us give freely to others.

The law of attraction compels us to think intensely, creatively and abundantly. It's from our thinking that we create our abundance. It is then manifested outwardly. We build human hearts as we shareour ideas, substance, wisdom and encouragement. A society of ideas, wisdom, peace, good human connections and opportunities, is a society of abundance. Success staff, in "11 ways to attract abundance in your life" [p.3] makes an allusion to the fact that when you stand at the beach and watch the waves hit the shore, do you think there is an end to the water? There is not of course, but we can't comprehend it, so we think the water is endlessly abundant. You would never deny a bucket full to a child building a sand castle because you can refile the bucket again and again. That's how the abundance mind works. You give away praise, ideas, recognition, knowledge and money because you know there is plenty to go round. What you give away will come back to you a thousand times over.

What we must remind ourselves about is that it is impossible to think lack and then experience prosperity.If we want prosperity and wealth, our thoughts must be in alignment with our highest goals or with our vision-prosperity and wealth. This is because everything that exists is created twice, first in the mind and then in reality. So, what we think and place our highest hopes and belief on is what we receive. Therefore,if we think lack, our minds throw away any other possibility and concentrate on lack.This is the source of scarcity and poverty. Our abundance is therefore,the result of abundance thinking manifested in reality. That is why we cannot think lack and experience a flood of prosperity. This is a contradiction in the law of attraction. Therefore, our thoughts must always be in alignment with our highest ideals and purposes.

What we receive from this difficult world cannot be anything more or less than what we think in our hearts, feel and speak to our lives. We therefore, must always nurture thoughts of abundance in our hearts as we expect abundance to manifest in our world. This is the real source of abundance as revealed by the law of attraction of abundance. Bobbi Anderson, in "effortlessly attract abundance," [p 1] maintains that if your goal is to build a business that effortlessly attracts prosperity and abundance, you have to ensure that you think often, feel, speak and imagine in a way that is in alignment with a prosperous and abundant existence.

According to the law of attraction, abundance requires that we change our mentality and mindset of lack and acquire the mindset that appreciatesand attracts prosperity and abundance. This is because abundance resides in the mind. It is our positive mindset that manifests abundance in our world. This mindset must be full to the brim with gratitude for what we possess.It is open, hopeful and able to share. It sees the universe as very rich and abundant in human supplies. Everyone that lives in the world could be sufficiently fed, beautifully clothed and effectively housed. Our problem is but hatred, greed, self-interest and hoarding. This greed and hoarding constitute what brings dissatisfaction in our lives. It incites and lures us to want more and more but achieving no fulfillment and satisfaction in our hearts.

It may not surprise anyone that we still find dejection, rejection, frustration, suicide, suicidal attempts and lack of fulfillment in the lives of those who have succeeded remarkablyin their lofty goals and big dreams. This occurs because they mistakenly seek satisfaction and fulfillment in the achievement of their goals and in the success of their dreams. Satisfaction and fulfilment are our possession independent of our achievement and comes from the mindset of abundance. Success, substance and wealth do not automatically put into our hearts the mindset of abundance. It is important to develop a mindset of abundance because it is here that satisfaction, fulfillment, joy and happiness are lodged, not in substance, wealth, position or influence.

I do not mean to down play on success and achievement for we all need to succeed in all that our hands find to do. The abundance mentality is a success mentality. It is positive, proactive, and expansive.This is the characterization of a mentality that is pro-achievement and success. The problem here is that those who succeed without the mindset of abundancemisplace their priorities and treasure the feeling that satisfaction and fulfillment come from achievement and success. This is an illusion that is common to most people. Our satisfaction, happiness, abundance and fulfillment come from within us. These values can be manifested in our lives even without the achievement of any goals.

These values dwell in the hearts of those filled with theabundance mindset or a positive mental attitude. ''Attracting prosperity and abundance-living dreams'' [p. 2] maintains that when you find real abundance, it is not going to require that you climb the corporate ladder or win the lottery. It doesn't tell you that you generate wealth through shrewd investment methods or start a new business. Simply because those things do not reflect authentic abundance. You'll have the capability to experience abundance and prosperity on every level and not only financial wealth. When this shift is complete, you'll discover abundance in the simplest of life's pleasures. The gaping hole in your mind is going to be finally filled and you will not feel the urge or need to acquire things before feeling abundance.

CREATING AND NURTURING ABUNDANCE

We humans are very concerned about living our lives in abundance. As indicated elsewhere, abundance is made possible by the generous hand of the creator. When we make our request to the creator, we don't just sit and fold our hands. We also have our own part to play in the creation of abundance. The universe rewards action. Abundance in our society does not come from the blue. It is therefore unthinkable that mankind should sit idly and wait for abundanceto land from space. We must conceive abundance in our mind and in substanceas a way to create and enjoy more. Our abundance in mind and substance should come from our effort in the creation process. Webster defines abundance as generating an ample quantity. The people must therefore create and nurture their abundance for no society ever reaps from where they never sowed. It is from our energy,plans, vision, dreams, intelligence and hard work that we create a society of plenitude, self-sufficiency and abundance.

The law of abundance is a human conviction that what the human mind can conceive and believe, the mind can achieve. And when we think victory, we get victory.Therefore, the mindset that we carry along is so important in creating and nurturing our abundance. Just like maintaining a mindset of abundance, action is so important and critical in creating abundance because the universe rewards action.Our hard work creates and nurtures our abundance. An example to follow is the American abundance, it is the result of exceptional hard work, intelligence and a positive mindset. As David Brooks, in ''why the USA will always be rich,'' 2002 [p.6] points out, that the most obvious feature of the land of abundance is that people work feverishly hard and cram their lives insanely full. That's because the candies are all around, they look up and plead to them, ''taste me, taste me, taste me.'' People in this realm live in perpetual aspirational truancy. They are bombarded from first waking to night time's last thought by images, messages, novelties, improvements and tales of wonders.

The desire to create and nurture an abundance society urges individuals to get involved in risk taking with determination and hope. Most poor societies are poor because individuals in them fear risks and play safe. Without undertaking risky ventures, we cannot grow, develop, change and create a society of plenty and abundance. It is when the society offers opportunities for risky ventures to individuals who can bear risks,create change and growth that the development process can be accelerated and abundancemade available in their society. This takes place in all aspects of their society-peace, security, food, travel, transportation infrastructure, education, health, human rights and freedoms, spirituality, laws and good governance.

In addition to material abundance, our societiesmustalso enjoy happiness, fulfillment and satisfaction. The point here is that we must develop our inner selves to march withthe level of our achievement. Our values must also prove to us that we have made achievements. Abundance therefore doesn't refer only to material substance but to all values that bring satisfaction and fulfillment to human life. When we are committed to inculcating technical, professional and general education into the minds of members of our society, we are in effect building minds. These minds will be capable of producing abundance in ideas, substance, knowledge, competencies, advice, encouragement, leadership and skills in all areas of human endeavors. These produce more abundance for our societies and the ripple effect continues.

To succeed to create these good qualities and values in our society, some people must be ready toventure.Our society will only change and develop as citizens gain more of the above values. Without this spirit in the hearts of members in our society, we can achieve very little. David Brooks, in "why the USA will always be rich," 2002 [p 7] submits that the environment of abundance accounts for energy, creativity and dynamism that mark national life. The lure of plenty that pervades the landscape encourages risks and adventure. The more opportunity there is and lies around, the more you will risk going for it and the less chance there is to go for it and fail.......

What soever we desire, when we pray;if we believe that we have it, we will have it. We cannot have what we do not want.If we aspire to experience and enjoythe inner or outer abundance, our minds must be abundant. It is not a matter to just float ourselves in substance and enjoy what is available. Our minds must first be rich in abundance. This must be the situation so that we are not like most people who have acquired great substance but are filled to the brim with scarcity and lack. These people cultivate and exercise greed, jealousy, stinginess, hoarding and backstabbing. In other words, their stores, bans and pockets are full but with their hearts and minds empty. They have succeeded remarkably in their goals, plans, visions and dreams but arein deficit of satisfaction,happiness and fulfillment. We must be reminded that while substance is necessary for ease and good quality of life, this is not the whole picture. Substance is an aspect of outer abundance which must be complimented by the inner abundance to trigger our feeling of satisfaction, happiness and fulfillment.

Most of our achievements are means to our ends and not ends in themselves. In other words, when we acquire wealth, power, position and influence, these are for us to be able to serve mankind fully, adequately and satisfactorily, thereby spreading abundance in our society. We fail in this mission when we substitute means for ends. We cannot enjoy our achievements greedily, stingily and selfishly and then expect joy, satisfaction, happiness and fulfillment in our life. In the law of attraction, we give first before it comes back to us in greater quantities. When we wallow in wealth and still hoard and jealous, it's because we lack the abundance mindset which is characterized by sharing, caring, solidarity and cooperation.

Inner abundance is independent of substance or the material environment. It comes from a mindset rich in solidarity, the human spirit, human interdependence, cooperation and mutuality, appreciation, gratitude and social inclusion. Real abundance is lodged in our minds. Noctis Enoch, in "the greatest secrets of life and reality revealed," [p. 1] submits that ....In order to experience abundance, you have to be abundant. Abundance is your true nature and when you think, act and live according to it, you will manifest abundance. The rich in mentality get richer while the poor in mentality get poorer. The accumulation of material wealth begins with wealth consciousness. To pursue spiritual development before you workon wealth creation is the key to attain both inner and outer riches.

Those who create abundance are therefore those who are rich in inner and outer abundance. It is possible for those who are rich in inner abundance to share abundance, for they can share their giftedness, competence, abilities, encouragement, advice, love and connectedness. Those rich only in outer abundance or substance will hoard and present stinginess, jealousy, egoism and self-interest. Those who experience and share abundance are rich in inner and outer abundance. When you lack inner abundance, you lack the qualities of human connectedness, solidarity, interdependence, cooperation and mutuality. When these qualities are absent, whatever you have belongs to you alone. Therefore, it's not possible to share outer abundance without inner abundance because the values of outer abundance don't permit you to share, care or engage in solidarity. To share, care and exhibit solidarity is contrary to the spirit of greed, stinginess, jealousy and hatred. The values of inner and outer abundance are opposed to each other.

Without the spirit of solidarity, cooperation and mutuality, there can be no talk of abundance.Human abundance can only be expressed in their ability to share,care and lift each other out of stressful situations and foster an inclusive society. It is for this reason that

David Brooks, in "why USA will always berich "2002 [p 8] submits again, that as people get more affluent, they are more likely to join community associations. They are more likely to care about the quality-of-life issues. They are more likely to call themselves environmentalists and they have the means to go off and explore our increasingly overcrowded parks.

In order to create and nurture our abundance, we must be ready to give off our old beliefs, values and the negative mindset. They are old because they donot serve us as they should. We cannot rise above our negative beliefs, values and mindset. The mindset constructed by limiting beliefs and values will not create and nurture abundance. The mindset that is unsure, undecided, fearful, procrastinating and embraces scarcity and lack, is certainly a limiting mindset.Such a mindset must be discarded for it cannot serve us in our development process. Embrace and nurture the mindset that convinces you that you are equipped, empowered, anointed and adequate to face your future. The creator equipped all humans with capabilities, potentials, abilities and competencies that they will ever need to accomplish the assignment of their destiny. The human being is truly, heavily loaded and sufficiently equipped for his assignment here on earth. But he must be assisted by his society to develop his potentials into productive skills, competencies and knowledge useful to him and his society.

Every human being has a life purpose, a particular assignment deposited in their spirit. In addition to this, God empowers, anoints, equips and loads all mankind to be able to accomplish their life purpose on earth. This empowerment and anointing, prepare and strengthenthem to be able to contribute their share to make the world a better place to be. If we fail to embrace or nurture this mindset, we may exist but cannot impact our planet. There will be no traces about our being here on planet earth. ''What does living in abundance mean?'' 2020 [p 3] makes the point that .... abundance thinking relies on our willingness to change our patterns of thought and make space for new ones. It also requires us to let go off past beliefs and assumptions and the openness to take on board new evidence and ideas.............Research has disproved many of the things we previously thought were true to be wrong.

Abundance is also created and nurtured when we re-invent ourselves as we sharpen, develop, and deploy our skills and abilities. Our skills, abilities and competencies attract and invitegreat opportunities to us as they show up in our life time. When we fail to sharpen ourpotentials into skills and abilities, we cannot see the opportunities that are open to us. It will therefore be so difficult to create abundance. As we fit ourselves squarely into these opportunities and utilize them effectively, we expand our world and our resources. This expansion creates more opportunities and abundance. Abundance is therefore created as we develop ourselves and employ our skills productively. When we become passionate in the use of our skills to contribute to human development, we expand abundance for humanity. Under this condition, we make our world a better place to be born, live and die.

Every human being has the built-in capacity to create a society of plenty. We also possess the ability to expand the stock of abundance and bring satisfaction, happiness and fulfillment to all. God endowed us with this capacity. Terri Maxwell, in ''abundance; building the life you want,'' [p 2] makes the point that he learnt that in order to create abundance, he has to give up the quest for money and instead seek meaning. As he focuses on what matters and what he is passionate about, money flows easily. When he looksfor meaningful work, it means he enjoys the work and, in the process, attracts more money. This is why passion comes in. To tap into abundance, we must be passionate about our work. Passion fuels abundance.

As this section rounds up, it is important to emphasize that the mindset and passion for work are leading issues that expand abundance and make it available to all. Without an abundance mindset, we can wallow in great abundance and still feel a lot of frustration, intimidation, scarcity and lack. When we put on the lack mindset, we don't see abundance anymore, notwithstanding its presence, nor can we share it. Again, without passion for work by all in our community, noabundance can be created. We might want abundance but it is the passion for work by all, that makes abundance available to all. We cannot have what we are not passionate about. Chance events, luck and coincidences may throw things at us [if at all they do].But in most cases such things do not amount to anything much and cannot satisfy. Surely, theyare far less than the abundance that our societies aspire to achieve.Of course, luck is a rare occurrence, it's our action that is rewarded.

We can only remind ourselves that of all the issues discussed in this section, we can build on the fact that theabundance mindset we put on and the passion for work are two leading factors that create our abundance. We have also been reminded that abundance is 'a mindset issue.' It's developed through the humanizing factors of solidarity, connectedness, sharing, caring, fellowship, gratitude, appreciation, cooperation and mutuality. David Brooks, "in why the USA will always be rich," [p 4] submits that the abundance mentality starts with the conscious premise that there exists at all times, close by, a happy hunting ground, a valley where diamonds are there just for the picking. In the land of abundance, work is worth it because it is often rewarded. In the land of abundance, a person's lower-class status is temporary. If the complete idiot next door has managed to pull himself up to the realm of Lexus driver, why shouldn't the same happen to you or me?

CHAPTER EIGHT

THE MINDSET OF ABUNDANCE

The mindset is such an Important and empowering concept in human live.We must not take it lightly for it is a leading issue in human development. But if we fail to build it strong with empowering valuesthat are positive and proactive, we are likely to fail in our priorities. It is imperative to examine the scripts, past and present that have gripped and are directing our mindset. The mindset rewards us fittingly. But does so, onlyif wepay great attention to theexaminationof the scripts that have tightly gripped it. These scripts may either be discarded, reinforcedor rescripted. Our failure or successall dependon the scripts that underlie, tightly grip and control our mindset. Some of the scripts in our mindset can pull us down, or weaken our legs even before we start our life's journey.

We are bombarded by expressions such as these on a daily basis:don't worry for hard work, no member of your family is up to anything; your grandfather was very unlucky and you will not be different; the world is so difficult that people like you cannot succeed out there. If we cannot wipe out all these negatives and rescript our mindset with positive, energizing, empowering, hopeful and achieving scripts, we could be lost forever.Therefore, building a positive mindset is such a worthwhile human endeavor that mustnot be considered lightly.For such a negative mindset as above,if we could inject into it values such as; hope and determination, hard work, self-confidence, self-disciplineand the winning spirit, it will assume apositiveorientation. A positive mindset underpins and fosters the abundance mindset.

The human being is altogether his mindset and when it is poorly or negatively scripted, he loses the battle with life before it begins. The mindset of abundance is hopeful, expansive, enduring, positive, resilient and inclusive. It builds the owner strong inside, so that he can build his world around him solid and amazing. Abundance is a state of mind that exudes positivism, solidarity, cooperation and mutuality, plenitude, amplitude and expansiveness. It is for this reason that Nicolette Stinson, in" 10 steps to develop an abundance mindset," 2019 [p 1] makes the point that your mindset can radically affect the course of your life. Overwhelming research on mindset shows that the way you think about yourself and the world around you can drastically change the way you learn, how you handle stress, how you create success, your resilience and even how your immune system functions.

We cannot be able to over stress the overwhelming importance of possessing and maintaining a mindset of abundance. The mindset of abundance is the win-win mindset. It is not egoistic, jealous, stingy, hoarding or selfish. It is the opposite of the win-lose mentality. It is but outgoing, proactive, appreciative, grateful, expansive and inclusive. It builds the oneness of mankind and considers that all should benefit from what God has made available for mankind. It considers that no one should win at the expense of others.It maintains that all should feel impressed and satisfied with the solution, agreement or decision that is made in any situation. Such a mindsetis anxious to expand and therefore it promotes research to innovate, improve, expand and recreate for the benefit of all mankind. This mindset always works tirelessly to ensure that whatever decision that is arrived at, is satisfactory and impresses all the parties involved and that no one wins at the expense of the other person, people or the community.

People with the mindset of abundance are a gift to societyand regrettably, such people are very few in number in our societies.This is why abundance is still a dream in our societies. In their effort to create abundance, they bring peace, security and development to the communities. The abundance mindset is aninclusive mindset for it always thinks about abundance and the wellbeing of all. It is built on fairness and equality. Nicolette Stinson, in "10 ways to develop an abundance mindset," [p 3] makes the point that creating an abundance mindset allows us to live an unlimiting, full and satisfying life; exude happiness despite circumstances; give and receive affection and items of high value with ease; feel plentiful, creative and inspired; take full advantage of and enjoy new opportunities that come our way; create memorable and meaningful life experiences ; feelsecure and confident in our life endeavors and create successful outcomes.

The mindset of abundance is a mindset of appreciation, gratitude and thanksgiving. When people are thankful, appreciative and hopeful, they enjoy untold happiness. This state of being multiplies abundance and makes the society enjoy more of the good life. Their communities are characterized by their desire to share, promote solidarity, cooperation and mutuality, human connectedness and the oneness of mankind. Under such conditions, there can be no lack, poverty, hatred or divisions. The citizens in a society of abundance feel free and relaxed. The stress in this society is not laid on substance, but strictly on solidarity, cooperation and mutuality, the ability to share, fellowship and exercise human interdependence. The abundance mindset therefore lays stress on a new way of living and a new approach to life. Here, the stress is laid on the fact that what God has provided is for all of us, it's adequate and can satisfy all. It is therefore the duty of the community to bring contentment and fulfillment to all.

The mindset of abundance is therefore a mindset of gratitude to God for he is the great provider and provides for all, with no exception. When we appreciate our abundance, its value and quality appreciate, multiply and there is always enough for all of us. Jessica DW, in ''how to shift from a scarcity to an abundance mindset,'' 2020, [p 3] submits that an abundance mindset always looks for gratitude. It's about our ability to see the positive and focus on what you already have. When you focus on the things you are grateful for, you naturally pull yourself out of the scarcity mindset. Gratitude is all about the appreciation for the good things in your life or the lessons you learnt along the way which help you cultivate an abundance mindset. The word 'appreciation' means increase in value. So, when you concentrate on the good feelings from the practice of gratitude, these positive feelings will increase.As they increase, so will the good things in your life.You will start to notice them more often. When you notice them, you can't help but feel more abundant.

In the acquisition, development and maintenance of this mindset of abundance, one important aspect is to surround oneself with like-minded people. People with mediocre minds suck you, praise you for what you can give them and finally make no contribution to your life. And then,you benefit nothing from their company. This is a company to avoid or they willcapture you over to mediocrity. Your company must be made up of people who move in your direction and to your destination. In the good company, there can be much to share together, learn, improve, develop and be mentally beneficial. It cannot be an overstatement to indicate here that people with an abundance mindset enjoy mutual benefits in that their minds, character and motivation rub off. Such people pull you up and share their future, motivation and aspiration with you, consciously or otherwise. Therefore, people with abundance mindsets get involved with and benefit only from people and activities that pull them to reach their destinations faster and successfully.

They may not make you feel important. But nevertheless, more than anything else, they deposit something important in your spirit.This deposit might set you thinking in fresh directions, to improve your life or change your course for the better. It will spur you to develop your potentials, capabilities and competencies. Caroline Castrillon, in "5 ways to go from a scarcity to an abundance mindset," 2020 [p 4] makes the point that we know those people who are always positive and see the glass as half-full instead of half-empty. Find them out and start to spend time with them. Attitudes rub off and if scarcity- minded people surround you, you will need to counteract that to make a career change. As Tony Robbins offers, the quality of a person's life is most often a direct reflection of the expectation of their peer group. Ask yourself if you look up to the people with whom you spend time, if not, you may need to search for othersthat live the life you aspire to.

To acquire and maintain the mindset of abundance, we must not forget to nourish our minds, body and spirit. It is when we nourish our minds and bodiesthat abundance can manifest. We must ensure our fitness through fitness exercises and good food. We must invest heavily and intentionally to train our minds to think and function in abundance. Mediocre mindsets cannot serve us in anyway. If we must create, innovate and produce enough for the abundance society, we must make the wise decision to protect our bodies, minds and souls. The nourishment of our souls is imperative, if we must achieve the abundance we want. Jo Ettles, in ''happiness the key to abundance-10 happiness tips,'' makes the point that we should invest in our wellness and practice self-care daily. We all need to nurture ourselves, emotionally, physically, spiritually and mentally. Feeling healthy naturally supports happiness. You have to take ownership of your journey, whether that be with your diet, your overall wellness, your fitness or just life in general. Self-care and making better choices in all areas of your wellness, empowers.If you want to feel real happiness, real joy, real energy, then take care of yourself.

The mindset of abundance is a mindset of possibilities and therefore it should be able to recognize and act on these possibilities. The mindset of abundance grips opportunities, possibilities, potentials and uses them to build a society that is full of abundance, more opportunities, possibilities and potentials. Abundance therefore builds and multiplies abundance. It makes the abundance society more abundant. The abundance mindset believes in abundance and then motivates and mobilizes the society to produce abundance and more of it -what you believe in, is what you receive.

The abundance mindset is open, liberal, creative, proactive, democratic, free and therefore sees and understands better. Anyone with the abundance mindset can therefore move freely towards their goal, plans, vision and dreams. It is for this reason that Caroline Castrillon, in "5 ways to go from scarcity to abundance mindset," [p 6] submits that an abundance mindset allows you to see more in your life: more options, more choices and more resources. When we focus on one particular thing very intently, other possibilities that are right in front of us go unnoticed. The brain can only absorb so much, so if your belief is, I can't do it or it's impossible, then any other thoughts contradicting that belief will get thrown out. Start training your mind to loosen its focus and create an expanding awareness. Ask yourself if you had all the time and money in the world and you knew you could not fail, what would you be doing?

CHAPTER NINE

THE SIGNIFICANCE OF AN ABUNDDANCE MINDSET

The mindset of abundance is the source of human expansion, happiness, fulfillment and attraction. It is not mysterious. When it's fully functional in man, it attracts things, people, opportunities,possibilities, affection and achievements. It's a mindset of appreciation, thankfulness, gratitude to others, nature and the creator. When you are filled to the brim with gratitude and appreciation, all good things are accessible to you. Our gratitude and appreciation invite the gratitude and appreciation of others and they respond in greater acts of kindness, love and concern, that creates more abundance. The abundance of our society doesn't appear from the blue. It comes from the carefully and intelligently planned, deliberate and intentional acts of men who are positive, outgoing, optimistic, upbeat and determined to build an abundance society.

People with an abundance mindset are happy, satisfied, fulfilled, relaxed and hardworking. They influence and impact society with positivism, optimism, enthusiasm and therefore create abundance. The mindset of abundance is infectious because it is admired, appreciated and talked about. It empowers people and overcomes challenges because it is not self-seeking or self-aggrandizing.Neither does it hoardnor is egoistic. It is outgoing. This kind of mindset is so significant to self and society as it is creative and productive. Jo Ettles, in "happiness- the key to abundance-10 happiness tips," makes the point that the power of a positive mindset can literally change your life. Make a habit to practice positivity. Ask yourself what kind of day you are going to have. Is it going to be a good or a great day? You create your mindset for the whole day by making a choice.If you choose to have what amazes you, you flood your whole body, mind and spirit with happiness.

The abundance mindset is a growth mindset. It encourages expansion, inclusion, plenitude, amplitude and abundance for one and all. It is my great wish that all societies embrace this perspective and enjoy the abundance that it produces. Without this mindset, society remains stagnant and sometimes regressive, rife with lack and scarcity, failure, disaster and the pandemic. The abundance mindset sees abundance in everything around. Whether it be success, failure, disaster, pandemic, inflation or depression,there is always some opportunity, possibility or some business to strike. In the mindset of abundance, nothing is wasted and nothing goes for nothing. When we become remorseful, miserable and regretful over our failures, we miss the mark because under this condition, we cannot draw out the learning and the fruitful experiences contained in our failures. When we through away our failures without exploiting them, we are at a great loss.

The abundance mindset is proactive, creates opportunities, faces and overcomes challenges and makes society a better place to be. Jarred Buch, in "uncertain futures and the importance of an abundance mindset," [p 2] makes the point that if you operate from a place of abundance, you know that they are always alternative solutions and methods to hit your goals and achieve the life you want. Whereas the scarcity mindset says, don't look for a better investment mix, a 4% return is steady and good, an abundance mindset knows that exploring a different mix can help you hack your future and achieve a greater sustainable growth. Abundance knows that the opportunity for greatness is out there, so long as you can do the work and research to earn it.

What is also important here is that wemustgreatly emphasize what an abundance mindset is not. We must never entertain in our hearts the mistaken thought that the abundance mentality is a mentality of complacency, laissez-fait, waywardness or provisions from the blue. You dare not sit idly, wait, hope and blame nature and circumstances. Certainly, God can provide for us from the blue, for he created the universe from nothing. But he has clearly informed us that those who do not work should not eat. He has also empowered us with knowledge, skill and power to meet our needs. The abundance mindset should therefore move us to greater engagement and high-level service in our calling, our profession, innovation, business, enterprise, technology, administration, law, politics, health and communication.

If we engage ourselves in a committed way in these areas of our endeavor, our abundance will be created and a society and life of abundance will be ushered in. The first step is to appropriate the mindset of abundance for everything begins in the mind. Jarred Buch, "in uncertain futures and the importance of the abundance mindset," [p1] submits that an abundance mindset is not an expectation that things will turn out to be okay on their own or that prosperity will fall into our laps. It is not complacency, laziness or blind acceptance. Too many that jump into the bandwagon of abundance seem to believe it means the world will provide success regardless of effort and commitment. And that just isn't true.

The mindset of abundance is a mindset of encouragement, support, collaboration and gratitude. It builds confidence in others and liftsthem up to higher ground. It is does not jealous,envy, backstab,discourageoris stingy. We create abundance by our openness. We must encourage, invest in people and help them to take risks and succeed. It is our duty to point others to opportunities and possibilities. It pays a lot to exercisegenerosityin praise, appreciation, gratitude, correction and warmth. Those values are important and build human connectedness, solidarity and the oneness of mankind. This is because mankind as the human family, is made to connect, share and fellowship. The abundance mindset lavishes others with praise and gratitude. It lavishly celebrates and welcomes the joy that comes withthe success of other members of society,just as well as our own success.

Jealousy, backstabbing, egoism, discouragement and dissatisfaction with other's success have built and maintained the society of lack, scarcity and misery. We must distance ourselves from these values that have nurtured meanness, poverty and underdevelopment.Sure, it has left our societies in poverty and misery. People with the abundance mindset search in their society to spur, encourage, support and lift up those who aspire to advance. This is how to make our societies abundant. This is how we can fill our societies with plenty and great quantities of whatever will bring satisfaction, happiness, fulfillment, joy, peace and security. Nicolette Stinson, in ''10 steps to develop an abundance mindset and mentality,'' 2019 [p7] makes the point that when a friend or acquaintance receives an accolade, reward or success, instead of trying to seethe with jealousy, or compare ourselves to them and wonder why welack, can we instead wish them genuine happiness and peace? Can we celebrate their accomplishment in our own hearts?

The mindset of abundance is characterized by the desire to give,share and support others. We may support otherswith whatever is available to build and lift them up to the mainstream of our society. When we Give substance it's important, but life is not all limited to substance. We may give our time, advice, an encouragement or spur them up in one way or the other. This may be enough to lift up your neighbor or colleague trapped in a scarcity mindset. You may share knowledge, skill, information and advice to help others learn, grow and be abundant. When we give our knowledge or substance, we grow richer and wiser for no one ever diminished by giving. Whatever we give, multiplies and comes back to us. A stingy, jealous and egoistic society is a nursery for lack, scarcity and misery. The results of this kind of society show up in later generations in poverty, misery, inequality and social exclusion.

When we share our blessings with our society,the sharing enhances the abundance mindset and creates a society of ample supply, and abundance. As we share, this enhances gratitude, appreciation, happiness, cooperation and mutuality, solidarity and the oneness of mankind. Therefore, if weshare our gifts, substance, ideas, knowledge and information it leads to personal development and social advancement.This is an effort to create the society we aspire to live in. Liz Windisch, in "why is adopting an abundance mindset important? " [p 6] makes the point that no one has ever become poor by giving. When you start to appreciate all that you have, you begin giving freely to others. As you enhance the lives of people around you, it benefits you also. It's a wonderful feeling to share with family and friends. But being generous and giving freely to others in need is very fulfilling to our hearts.

The mindset of abundance is also characterized by a sense of abundance for all. Whatever is available is never limited or in short supply. For in the mind of the sharer, there is the possibility to share with all who are present, whatever is available to share. When we have the spirit to share, we do not lack. All human beings need our help. The win-win spirit is the spirit that enhances social harmony and gives a feeling of satisfaction, happiness and fulfillment. There is no sense for us to win the argument just to lose our partner. It pays us a lot to win our partner and lose the argument, if possible. And more also, if we could win the argument and still keep our partner.We must be concerned and involved in the enhancementof harmony and satisfaction among our people. The win-lose spirit is a characteristic of the lack and scarcity mindset. Under this condition whatever is available is never going to go round. Why?Because the 'giants'take their lion's share and leave only the crumps, inadequate for the majority or the ordinary people.

The mindset of abundance is a mindset of social justice, fairness, equality and human concern.These are the values that create and maintain abundance and when they pre-occupy the hearts of humans in any society, they exude abundance, plenitude and amplitude. Caroline Castillon, in ''5 ways to go from scarcity to abundance mindset,'' 2020 [p 5] the point is made that the scarcity mindset believes that if one person wins another loses. Try to create a win- win in your life to combat this manner of thought. Look for ways for both parties to leave with a sense of accomplishment and a better feeling about the relationship. Consider this practice in both your personal and professional life. This often means to listen without judgement or censorship and fully understand what a win- win means for both of you and brainstorm solutions until you find one that satisfies both of you.

CHAPTER TEN

DOES ABUNDANCE PRODUCE HAPPINESS, SATISFACTION ANDFULFILLMENT?

The question to answer here is whether our happiness, satisfaction and fulfillment are products of our abundance.These human qualitiesconstitute the goal for all aspiring human beings and their societies. These values are qualities of the mind and function independently of the surrounding circumstances. But no one argues the fact that our happiness, satisfaction and fulfillment can be greatly dampened by ill-health, the death of a loved one, our embarrassment from killings in war or human misery. But those who have already nurtured these qualities in their minds can only have them lightly affectedby these circumstances, not eliminated. Happiness, satisfaction and fulfillment in people, are there not because of the circumstances but in spite of them. We can most likely admire this scenario, where a man is rejected and mishandled by the circumstances in his environment, in his family, nation or his profession but remains solid in his happiness, satisfaction and fulfillment. Such a man is made of the sterner stuff andhas the mindset of abundance. He is an example to follow.

The values of happiness, satisfaction and fulfillment have already been built into all human minds. When our society produces abundance in substance, wisdom, peace, security and social wellbeing, the good life is enhanced and society is moved up to higher level. Without the abundance mindset, the abundance of society will be consumed greedily, stingily or hoarded. In this way we reduce our communities down to societies of lack, scarcity and poverty. Therefore, abundance produces happiness, satisfaction and fulfillment only on condition that the members of society already have the mindset of abundance characterized by caring, sharing, solidarity and interdependence. Substance or wealth are not enough to fill the hearts of people with happiness, satisfaction and fulfillment.

Happiness, satisfaction and fulfillment are cognitive qualities lodged in the mind and are alwaysexercised by very few people. We no doubt are very aware of people who have made very great and remarkable achievements, commanded great power and influence and with very great substance, who have but empty hearts, completely void of happiness, satisfaction, fulfillment, joy or enthusiasm. They ponder and wish they could be happier, fulfilled and satisfied. This is the result of the absence of an abundance mindset. Ben G Yacobi, in "life and the pursuit of happiness, "2015 [p 85] makes the point that in Nicomathean Ethics, Aristotle outlines the notion of virtue, happiness and the good life, and he concludes that humans have a natural desire for knowledge, God, happiness, society and the good life is one that satisfies them fully. For Aristotle, happiness is not pleasure or having material things, but it is about self-fulfillment and to live in accordance with virtue, furthermore, happiness is not a temporary state but a goal in life............

Happiness is a state of joy and contentment and is the aspiration of all mankind. Everyone wants to attain this higher dimension of fulfillment and satisfaction and the problem is how to get there. It would appear there are some parameters to be met. But in actual fact, it's a matter of shifting our mental gears. Since happiness, satisfaction and fulfilment are cognitive qualities that describe the state of our mindset, we simply have to assign the mind to produce these qualities as need be. If you want happiness, satisfaction and fulfillment, just make up your mind to enjoy these virtues. Be it in your job, your family, your acquaintances, friends, country or your entire life here on this planet. These values are important for success towards your goals, plans, dreamsor your entire life. If you wait to access your satisfaction, happiness and fulfillment through substance, power, position and influence, you have failed. Why? because even those whopossess all these important factors still ask the question, is this all to it? Is this all about the life? Is this all there is? Where is the happiness, satisfaction and fulfillment in life? They are still in search of these qualities and press on for more achievements in search of happiness and satisfaction.

There is a void, some emptiness that can only be filled by the presence of the creator who longs to occupy the first place in our lives and in our hearts. Ben G Yacobi, in ''life and the pursuit of happiness,'' [p 85] makes the point that ....the goal in life is to achieve happiness and the most satisfying life includes simple pleasures, tranquility, moderation and intellectual contemplation. Whereas unsatisfied material desires are the source of unhappiness, natural desires are easily satisfied. Thus, one should refrain from excessive and vain desires such as wealth, power and fame which have no limit and are hard to satisfy. This removes the strain and worry of expectation and possible failure to fulfill these desires...............happiness comes from inner peace of mind and not from external things.

Because of the struggle for happiness, satisfaction and fulfillment, through the acquisition of substance, power, position and influence, life is seemingly a zero-sum game or a win-lose encounter. This is not the way things should be. The zero-sum game approach cannot develop our society because it is exclusive and limiting. A society in which when one man gains others must lose. This certainly, is far from the society of abundance. Abundance means win-win, expansion, inclusion, access to opportunities, possibilities and potentials for all. A society of abundance is underpinned by resourceful, creative, energetic and competent people. They are alsoproactive, cooperative and change-oriented.

The society of abundance is endowed with people armed with new values. Values that enhance productivity, creativity, solidarity, the win-win spirit, cooperation and mutuality. Richard Layard, in ''promoting happiness ethics: the greatest human principle,'' submits that in this world individuals do collaborate sometimes but only when it is to their own individual interest. There is no concept of the common good and life is largely a struggle on the ladder of success. But such a struggle is a zero-sum game since if one person rises another must fall. In such a world it is impossible that all should progress. Instead, if all are to progress, it has to be a positive-sum game where success for one brings success for others.

The mindset ofabundance produces happiness, satisfaction and fulfillment. But this is the caseonly when it's underpinned by an atmosphere of gratitude, solidarity, human oneness, the spirit ofsharing, appreciation and a harmonny. These are humanizing qualities that govern the mindset of abundance. All human beings are wired to connect with each other. This social connection is altogether animated by the spirit of gratitude for who we are and have.It is also animated by the appreciation for other's kindness to us.Abundance also means the enriching and harmonious relationship with members of the society. This kind of atmosphere in our society will certainly produce happiness, satisfaction and fulfillment in our lives. We give our gratitude and appreciation to our society for having made us to be who we are. We make our contribution for our social advancement and see the good results in our society. This brings to our hearts the happiness, satisfaction and fulfillment that we need.

Most of our societies are characterized by a jealous mentality, egoistic tendencies and self-seeking. Such societies are rife with the scarcity mindsets, negative mentalities and limiting circumstances. In these societies, scarcity, poverty, misery and hardship are rife. The high ideals of happiness, satisfaction and fulfillment are rare and far from these societies. Mark Petit, in '' 7 ways an abundance mindset makes your life happier and more fulfilling," 2019 [p. 3] makes the point that grateful people practice the proactive gratitude. There is an appreciation for what they have and they are not envious of what others have. The key is to focus on who you are and what you have. It is all about expanding strength, expanding internal gratitude and appreciating the people you have in your life. If you go into any situation with a proactive and a gratitude mindset, you will always focus on what is great about the situation or people rather than what is wrong.

Abundance has the ability to bring happiness, satisfaction and fulfillment to human life. This happens evenwhere great wealth and power have failed and repeatedly failed. The abundance that brings happiness, satisfaction and fulfillment to the human life, is true abundance which is a harmonious mix between the inner and the outer abundance. Abundance is lodged in the mind and happiness, satisfaction and fulfillment are also lodged in the mind, for they are qualities of the mind. This is why men with great substance, power, position and influence without a mindset of abundance will continue to search for satisfaction, happiness, and fulfillment by adding more substance, power and influence. This of course is futility. What is also true is that even thoughsatisfaction, happiness and fulfillment are cognitive qualities, they are also temporary affected by the social and physical environment. Like when these qualities are dampened when we experience killing, the sufferings of refugees and the hungry. But this dampening is temporary.

The abundance that brings satisfaction, happiness and fulfillment is what some people call true abundance. The mind must be in harmony or in good relations with the environment in order to produce the abundance that will ensure happiness, satisfaction and fulfillment in life. In "what does true abundance and happiness mean to you?" [p 7] the point is made that ....real wealth and abundanceare not derived as a result of the attachment of money in and of itself. But real abundance, happiness and fulfillment in life, what I call real wealth is harmonizing the physical, financial, relational, emotional and spiritual aspects of life which enable you to experience real wealth.

I must make this abundantly clear; I have in no way tried to down play on substance, power, position and influence. As significant and great as we know them to be, they have their special place in the scheme of things. There is a lot of evidence that most people that have sleepless nights in search of satisfaction, happiness and fulfillment are in possession of substance, power and position. This brings to our attention the fact of the emptiness of wealth and substance. The achievement of our goals, plans, dreams and the acquisition of substance, power, position and influence are all so important. As important as they are,they have their own place in the scheme of things in our lives. We dare not think and dream that they should do what they cannot do. Our satisfaction and fulfillment should come from the fact that we dowhat we should do effectively with the people we so desire, at the time we should do and get the satisfactory results that we get.

Satisfaction and fulfillment come from the fact that we do what we enjoy doing. We do it so effectively with the peoplewe enjoy workingwith. We also do it at the time we enjoy our work.And then, we get satisfactory results. Here we have a pictureof what moves us to exercise our career. We have got to cooperate with those who also make a contribution to the development of society. Part of our satisfaction comes from the fruitful results that we get. Here, we do not see the dominance of power, substance, position and influence.

May be our desire should be to be effective in ourlives' purpose and enjoy the exercise ofour purpose with others. We must carry out this purpose in a timely manner with the desire to get the best results for humanity. In ''what does true abundance and happiness mean to you?'' [p 6] the point is made that so many in our world today believe that if only they could acquire a certain amount of money, that would be all they require to enjoy life. While it is true that money is an extremely important part of everyone's life in this day and age and required for survival, it certainly is not the cure-allthat creates and experiences a truly fulfilled life.

CHAPTER ELEVEN

AUTHENTIC HUMAN DEVELOPMENT PRODUCES AN ABUNDANCE SOCIETY

The society of abundance, the hope of allmankind, will come true as we effectively pursue it through the authentic human development process. It is through our development effort carried out authentically by all of us with all in mind that we will accomplish our goal of plenty, amplitude and great abundance. Authentic human development begins in the mind. This must be the abundance mindset that brims with the human spirit: human connectedness, solidarity, the oneness of mankind and social advancement.

If development is for man, how can we fail to involve him in his development? But we cannot have him fully integrated, committed and involved in his development if we fail to see him functioning as a member of his community. He is socially connected with other men, spiritually hinged to his creator, economically, politically and culturally actively involved and committed to build a society that will please, satisfy and give him fulfillment.

The creator of the universe can throw abundance at us, but in most cases, that is not what he does. Why? Because all things that we ask from the creator of the universe are received through our action. We ask and then God supplies through our action.Authentic human development is development with a human touch. It is a true, original and enduring development approach. It convinces all to participate in their advancement and to benefit therefrom. It's a development approach that is universal.It caters for all aspects of the human being and assists all to benefit from the process. Lori Kelleher, in authentic development, 2020 [p 2] makes the point that philosophical underpinnings of integral human development, holds that truly, authentic development requires not only that the poor be relieved of their poverty, but also that every person- rich or poor stands together with others in a relationship of solidarity as members of the human family.

Our past development experience has not been satisfactory. It failed totally to bring about human fulfillment and to ensure human happiness and wellbeing. Our solidarity, human fellowship, connectedness, social concern and the humanizing spirit have all been threatened and rendered doubtful. There has been an attempt at development but without these values to lead the way, our developmenthas certainly been a faultypursuit. It wouldn't work because there can be no human developmentwithout empowering and ennobling asocial values. The development process that puts the economy on the center and man at the periphery, is upside down. Such a process will lack human values and development that lacks human values is faulty. Past development therefore misplaced our priorities and failed to satisfy our desires.

When we can no longer entertain mediocrity, limiting beliefs or unempowering values and scripts because we have stepped up to higher and empowering beliefs and scripts- this is development of the highest order. We have moved forward and upward; we have expanded and are enjoying higher ideals. We are compelled and moved by the human spirit to share our ideals of cooperation and mutuality, human solidarity, interdependence and unity. This is the development pathway that has dethroned the economic development approach. The economic approach to development concentrated on wealth and substance to the exclusion of human values. There can be no development without these human empowering values and beliefs. The result is development without human satisfaction, happiness and fulfillment.

Development is first and foremost, a positive- mindset- issue. Whatever positive and satisfying achievement registered in the physical environment was first of all initiated, developed and expressed in the mind. After this initial expression, it was then extended to the physical environment.Real development will include our attachment to human solidarity, cooperation and mutuality, human fellowship, interdependence and unity. Annabel Shilson- Thomas, in ''authentic development [p 2] makes the point that by recognizing each other's needs and joining hands in solidarity, many women in the majority world, often model what authentic development means. They affirm each other's worth and are eager to embrace changes which bring greater fulfillment to the whole community, whether they work cooperatively, share resources or become the voice of peace.

The authentic human development process is charged with the responsibility to developthe human person andhis environment. This development paradigm is very inclusive. No one takes the arrogant posture to pretend to know what is good for others nor arrogates to himself the authentic development process that is underway in the community. The authentic human development process creates the abundance of the community. It is therefore, not "a one-man- affair." The entire community is mobilized to rise up, like one man, against the impediments of development in theirsociety.

This rising up is a learning process in which the people in their development process are all learning the values of solidarity, cooperation and mutuality, interdependence, the oneness of mankind through working as a team to achieve their abundance. The stress is laid on these values and standing together as members of their society. This approach is necessarybecause the development process that concentrates principally on economic development to the exclusion of humanizing values that make man human,has failed and repeated failed. For by it, most economies boom but the human predicament continues to grow worse. This proves that it has not work.

It is only when man is well adjusted and relaxed personally, socially, spiritually and culturally that he puts on his best to produce in industry, administration or business and other areas. Lori Keleher, "in authentic development," [p 2] submits that the position that every person benefits from participation in authentic development is inevitable and when we recall that integral human development is concerned with the development of the whole person in such a way that enables people to be more human where being more is distinct from having more. When this notion is taken seriously, it follows that economic and material resources are not the only benefits that emerge from the authentic development process.

The authentic development process is the source of abundance, it provides us with the resources that raise and enhance our quality of life. If we have to enjoy good health, be educated, well housed and enjoythe physical environment, the authentic development process makes this possible. We all come into our world adequately equipped, empowered and anointed for the assignment that God Himself puts into our hearts. Our society then assists us to develop our gifts, potentials and abilities. This enhancesthe release of our skills and competencies so that we become capable and can make use of the opportunitiesand possibilities in our environment. In other words, God puts into every human being the resources, adequate enough to participate in the creation of human abundance. In this way, He prepares manto makehis contribution to the economic, social, cultural, political andthe spiritualdevelopment of his society. Man must therefore take his own responsibility to sharpen his skills to enhance his success in his assignment. God therefore, is the ultimate creator of abundance in our society.

The authentic development process is the channel through which the abundance of our society is made available. Through this development process we can enhance the quality of our life and improve the situation of our physical environment. The ''encyclopedia of world problems, in "improving the quality of human life," [p 1]makes the point that the fundamental indicators of quality of life include having sufficient nutrition, adequate accommodation and environment, social and psychological fulfillment and health..............Individual, cultural and ideological perception of life quality will vary. It may be agreed that the quality of lifecan be achieved at any mode of existence as long as there is fulfillment of some or all of the above factors. By the same token, contemporary development is seen as the ability to improve the quality of life and the conditions of the above factors to enable people enjoy longer healthier and fulfilling lives.

The authentic development process has the abundance of society as its goal and the framework that makes this achievement possible is the social mobilization process. The whole society is encouraged, educated andempowered to get involved and committed in the development of their community. They are mobilized and empowered to be their own development agents for no one at a distance can tell them what is good for their society. But at a distance,they can support the development process with their substance, suggestions and ideas. They must not controlthe development machinery to their advantage. Their ideas, substance and the physical effort of members of society when organized and mobilized, can usher in effective and authentic human development. This cuts off the dependence on aid that has delayed and even killed the development initiative in our societies.

When people learn to be masters of their development, development becomes authentic, with the built-in ability to humanize, socialize, reward and bringmeaningto participants. They can happily and excitingly contribute to their achievements, plans, goals and dreams. Aid is not a thing to depend on but it is not bad if it comes to boost effort, encourage and assist in what our society members have put their hands together to do. What must be discouraged or stopped is societies' dependence on aid or waiting for support or initiative to come from elsewhere.

We cannot permit that people elsewhere should initiate and controlthe development of our societies from a distance. Lori Keleher, in "authentic development," 2020, [p 2] makes the point that the understanding of this development shifts the development paradigm away from the one in which aid, charity and service, flow one way from the rich givers to the poor beneficiaries or takers. Instead, within the integral human development perspective, authentic development integrates each and every person in a humanizing process of standing in relationships of solidarity as we strive together toward promoting the common good. The recognition of the human dignity of each person is both the means and the end of this process.

Authentic human development and abundance are important and leading issues in humanizing our society. Authentic human development means that the people have been self-mobilized and are capable of stemming the tide of the impediments to their development. Abundance also means that society has been effectively mobilized, empowered and equipped to produce.Under this condition, they can capture and utilize productively whatever opportunities are available to them.The society can now enjoy the abundance of substance, peace, security, services, products, solidarity, sharing, cooperation and mutuality, interdependence and connections.

Authentic human development therefore humanizes and makes our society a place for human beings. In such a society, men do not mind only their business they are also concerned about the success of others.They are also concerned with the growth, success and achievement of fellow members in their society. They are compelled as promoters of solidarity to encourage, share, support, educate and cooperate to enhance the success of all. They appreciate, enjoy and celebrate the success of all and everyone in their community, just as they celebrate their own.

In this society men and women learn the human values that help them to relate, share, fellowship andmakeall members their brothers' keepers. Annabel Shilson-Thomas, in "authentic human development," [p 2] submits that we are not created by God to live alone. Living in a community is an essential expression of who we are. But community does not just happen- it is something that men and women must work together to develop. A community needs a soul if it is to become a home for human beings. You the people, must give it this soul. Participation is a duty to be fulfilled, consciously and responsiblyby all, for the common good.

CHAPTER TWELVE

ABUNDANCE, THE ASPIRATION AND HOPE OF ALL MANKIND

It is an inborn quality in the human mind to gravitate towards a society, environment or place of abundance. Almost everybody wants to enjoy. But regrettably,the greater majority never care to think that what is to be enjoyed has been made available by the efforts of some members of society. We like the fruits of development and sometimes claim our rights to them, not even considering whether we made our contribution or not. This is a big issue, but again, even in the organized social structures,many escape the planification, organization and the execution stages of a projectand only show up at the level of benefits.

When a society is faced with this kind of problem, it's important to approach it with care, wisdom and a sense of love.This will reduce tension, the wounding of minds and destabilization of society. We must not forget that these are the same people who can be educated, encouraged and involved toparticipate activelyinthe development processes of their community. It is important to be gently firm and involve all in the community.They should be educated to see the need for all to be involved, committed and enthusiastic in creating an abundance society. We are encouraged to assist them to build their community in solidarity and create a great stock of abundance for all to benefit. More hands will do more work, making it lighter for all and in effect,create a greater stock of abundance for everyone.

Abundance ultimately comes from the creator's hand and is made available to mankind through the development process that is authentic. Those who are involved in this authentic development process have developed a mindset of abundance that is proactive and expansive. They exercise cooperation and mutuality, solidarity and the human spirit. When a community that fosters a mindset of abundance gets involved in authentic human development, the results are fantastic and far-reaching.

Those who have the values of authentic human development and endowed with a mindset of abundance, enjoy their society to the fullest. Their societies are characterized by interdependence, happiness, satisfaction, connectedness, peace, security and goods and services. This is why a society of abundance is the aspiration and hope of all mankind. This is a truly authentic human family. But most of the time we fail to put on the effort that brings this about and still expect to enjoy a society of abundance. The creator who makes all things available to us does not permit those who idle and take no part in the development process to take part in the benefits.

The law of abundance instills man with the mindset of abundance which empowers him to look beyond his hardship. Hardship may want to show up but he refuses to notice it. He does not nurse it nor give it anyattention. Why? Because his attention is focused on abundance. At the human realm, abundance can be viewed in two perspectives- the inner and the outer abundance. Inner abundance sees our hardship but encourages us to look further and see the bigger picture. It encourages us to work, hope, plan, dream and to be optimistic about our future. It reminds us about a new day that will bring a difference and make our hearts happy, satisfied and fulfilled. Inner abundance is an inner resource that comes from a positive mentality called ''the abundance mindset.'' It cannot fail because it is on the control. It thinks abundance, dreams abundance, plans abundance and hopes only abundance. Of course, our thinking coupled with our plans and dreams, make us what or who we are. Therefore, our abundance thoughts can make us and our society produce abundance.

Our outer abundance refers to substance or material resources, power, position, influenceand our wealth or achievements that affect our life style. Outer abundance is under the influence of the abundance mindset. Our mindset makes us who we are and have. Outer abundance is made available to complement our lives.''Creating abundance in a situation of poverty,'' [p6] submits that finally we must work towards an abundance mindset. This happens by consistently reminding ourselves to look for the blessing in our life even in the mist of difficult situations.

A society of abundance is a human society that has caught the dream andis determined to foster a positive mental attitude, enthusiasm, solidarity, a spirit of hope and determination. Mankind in this society is endowed with the feeling that we are born to connect with others, share, contribute, develop our society and enjoy human fellowship. This is the spirt of abundance which appreciates what is available, shows gratitude and anticipates what is yet to come. Gratitude and appreciation are manifestations of the mindset of abundance. Gratitude and appreciation for what we have and what belongs to others is the spirit that multiplies and expands our resources and makes them abundant. This attitude sees the resources of society as belonging to all members of society. These resources are meant for society's benefit, growth and expansion. They are not for self-interest, a particular group of people or for looting. For our society to developit must embrace this attitude for it is void of cheating, jealousy and hatred.

If we are all agreed that ultimately, God is the source of all abundance, it becomes necessary that we dig deep into God's heart to be informed of his purpose of makingabundanceavailable to mankind. When we respond appropriately to God's purpose of abundance to us, we create a society of abundance. The purpose of God's abundance to mankind is to bless man so that he in turn becomes a blessing to his society. What God gives us is always more than our requirements and his purpose is that we can use it to share, care, fellowship and connect with others. When we receive God's blessings and think and feel only about ourselves, we limit God's generosity and consequently the abundance of our society. In our own little way, we can use it to exercise our humanness to others who cross our path.

God rewards us generously through the assignments he gives us and we ought to make our society benefit from our substance, power, position and influence. God has lavished us with the mental and physical resources.Why? So that our society can enjoy abundance in every aspect of human life. Most of our societies have these human resources yet they cannot go round because we are unable to connect to each other at the human level. There is lack of solidarity, cooperation and mutuality, interdependence and fellowship. We are unable to connect because we continue to harbor thoughts of jealousy, hatredand greed. Dr. David Martins, in "the purpose of abundance," [p 1] maintains that God is looking for people who love to bless others. There is a big responsibility which comes with the gift of receiving. God doesn't pour his blessing into our lives that we become hoarders and heap up more and more treasures for ourselves.

Why don't we care about others? Why aren't we enthusiastic toshare with others? Why is there no solidarity and the ability to humanize our world? For all these questions the answer is simple. It's because we are in a 'competition.' We compete in our minds and physically with each other to have more, enjoy more, build more, bank more, travel more and hoard more. So that we are all-round giants. The human spirit is endowed with the desire to be richer, more powerful, better, looked up to and more respected than all around him. This seemingly is the source of all poverty. Why? Because those who are seemingly successful in the competitionhave already develop the capacity to hoard more, siphon more, embezzle more and corrupt more. I do not mean that all what we own is not authentically ours but to blame the evil that at times overpowers some people. Under these conditions there can be no abundance because what could have been ableto go round has been hoarded,misappropriated, mismanaged or banked out of society. We grip and hold tight to what would have been released to benefit mankind andmake our society abundant.

This is why individuality, self-interest and self-aggrandizement do not benefit our society for these values cannot create abundance in our society.May be these values have succeeded elsewhere.Surely,for those societies where inequality and social exclusion are entrenched, individuality, self-interest and self-aggrandizement have brought untold hardship and suffering to the majority of people. We see this as inequality and social exclusion are intensified. Meg McCracken, in "5 ways to discover purpose and abundance in a world that has forgotten," [p 3] makes the point that the message of lack is engrained in the very fabric of our society. Everywhere we turn we are being told to get more, be more, learn more, earn more etc. So, our sense of abundance is swallowed whole by all-consuming vortex of more, more,more, never enough. And we can't but feel the urge to continually fortify and fiercely protect what is me, my and mine.

In terms of abundance, our society still has so many missing pieces. These missing pieces refer especially to the value perspective. It is what needs to be inside us in order to make us abundant. It is therefore important to fill the empty spaces and measure up to an abundance society. An example of a missing piece in this package of abundance is the value of 'win-win.' This is what should build a society of abundance. The win-win value which should be the core value of abundance is principally about empathy, expansion, growth, equitable distribution and fairness in all our dealing with others. This mindset considers that what God has provided for society, tangible or intangible, inner or outer resources can always go round and bring happiness, satisfaction and fulfillment to all mankind.

The important thing here is to mobilize and gear people up for authentic human development which is the source of all abundance. Talking about the mindset that generates abundance, in "the importance of an abundance mindset," [p 3] the point is made that they think about how they can create more value in the world for others compared to competition. They are happy to hear about other's success and lift other people up around them and continuously encourage others to keep taking action.

Abundance is the aspiration and hope of all mankind for everyone enjoys a society of plenty, generosity, solidarity, cooperation and mutuality. It happens even though most people will not make their contribution to the success of this society. To Live in this society is likeshifting the gear leverof our car from one level to the other. The society'smindset must be shifted from lack to abundance. The abundance mindset generates positivism, a win-win mentality, growth, expansion and authentic human development.

It may not be the best society for competition and self-interest.The reason is that its characterizations are solidarity, interdependence, spirit of participation, sharing, caring, social inclusion, the common humanity of man and human connectedness. All these values are underpinned by the authentic human development process. This makes abundance available to all; creating a society that is the aspiration and hope of all mankind.

CHAPTER THIRTEEN

THE PURPOSE AND END OF ABUNDANCE

The concept of abundance, if given the opportunity, can work on effectively renewing and transforming our hearts and minds. It can assist us in bringing change to our world. The mindset of abundance when cultivated, nurtured and embraced, can produce a new society in our world. If we must be humans, then, we need the humanizing spirit that we lost. We must redefine ourselves and embrace the humanizing qualities that will make our society a place to be. Victory for anyone in our society should be appreciated and embraced as success for all members of society. The purpose of abundance is therefore to make our society embrace and enjoy mutual benefits, human solidarity, interdependence, inclusiveness, cooperation and mutuality and the human family spirit. These and more will make the abundance society enviable and sought after.

Our society must be humanly connected, socially integrated and able to enjoythe benefits of cooperation and mutuality, exercised by all. There must be social harmony and human concern.All these factors enhance the wellbeing of the human family. As human beings we are wired to connect with each other in order to nurture our humanness. Penny Tremblay, ''in abundance versus scarcity mentality,'' 2017 [p 1], submits that for the abundance mentality, victory means success that brings mutually beneficial results to all involved, it recognizes unlimited opportunities for positive growth and development. It realizes that there are three ways to do things: my way, your way and our way. It appreciates the uniqueness of others. The best way is our way because when two ways are combined, the result is more than double.

As we welcome and embrace the concept of the abundance mindset in our society and give opportunity for it to blossom and mature, our minds are shaped for good. It builds our minds to begin to think positively, feel,careand connect with others. Under this condition, we make our plans with others inclusive and live our lives together with them. Since we are connected with others and feel for them, our thinking now is'win-win.' Our challenges and theirs are one. When we win, they have won and when they lose, we have lost. When we rejoice, they rejoice and when they celebrate, we celebrate. A humanizing spirit has tied this society into a single gamut of love and human concern.

Under this condition, we can say that what is mine is yours, and what is yours is mine. The ability to share, care, enhance interdependence, solidarity and cooperation increases. And these are the values that prevail in our community. Everyone in our society wants to share their ability, capability, substance, power,position and influence. Under this condition, the society is fertile with substance, peace, security, wealth, opportunities and possibilities.

Penny Tremblay, in "abundance versus scarcity mentality," 2017 [p 2] poses the question, what would our lives be like if we changed our thinking to be in sync with a mentality of abundance? Examples of this mindset would be to believe that the world has fruits for all, that there is plenty to go round, that there is a lot of room at the top and that we are beneath no one and superior to no one. If we would develop this mentality, we would free ourselves from fear, we would be immune to criticism and we would experience ultimate freedom in our minds and in our hearts.

The mindset of abundance creates opportunities for members of society to display their talents, abilities, potentials, gifts and competencies for the benefit of their community. Every community has its men of talents, business skills, energetic and enterprising people, innovators, entertainers, sculptors, engineers, religious leaders, sportsmen and educators. These and more, are the source of the abundance of our societies, for every community is endowed with a good supply of men and women armed with these skills. With these human resources available in every community, our society can expand and influence their supply of abundance. It happens when these men and women armed with skills, rise up to take their assignment in the framework of authentic human development. Abundance is created with the mindset of expansion, positivity, proactiveness and social inclusion. In "discover the power of thought in creating abundance and happiness," [p 5] the point is made that what is crucial for us to understand is this, if we chose to have an abundant, happy, balanced and harmonious life, a kind and quality of life that the vast majority don't, our predominant thoughts need to be focused on and in harmony with what is desired not what is lacking.

When abundance is created, the expectation is that the members of society will enjoy happiness, satisfaction and fulfillment. The quality of life improves and society lives at a higher level. There is also the assumptionthat the society that has abundance is a society of people with the abundance mentality. It is also assumed that this society imbibes and nurtures the humanizing spirit that enhances solidarity, interdependence, cooperation and mutuality. It is not pregnant with jealousy, greed, backstabbing and envy. It has good feelings for all, it's socially inclusive and makes the benefits of development accrue to all.

The abundance mindset is therefore an approach that nurtures authentic human development. The point is wonderfully made in ''abundance versus scarcity mindset.''2017 [p 2] When it comes to human interaction, characteristics of integrity and maturity, an abundance mentality has the ability to create a win- win situation for all parties involved. Win-win is a thought process in which both the mind and the heart continuously seek mutual benefit in human interaction. With the win-win frame of mind, all parties involved feel good about the solution, agreement and the decision, because there are mutually beneficial for everyone involved. In this way of thinking, emphasis is put on cooperation, not competition.

The great message established in this work is that all abundance flows from the creator whose purpose is to bless man so that he can be a blessing to his society. Therefore, the purpose of abundance is that itblesses the entire community. Unfortunately, hoarding, greediness and stinginessare all negative values which are responsible for scarcity, lack and poverty. These negative values have tightly gripped our societies and trapped them in lack. These negative values also do well to multiply theirpoverty and misery. The creator's intention is that no one will suffer the scourge of poverty and misery. But because of human greed and self-interest that are rife in our society,we experience untold suffering from scarcity and lack in our society. God put it very clearly and vividly in the Holy Scriptures,in the book of Jerimiah 29,11, ''I know the plans I have for you, plans to prosper you and not to harm you. There are plans to give you a hope and a future.

There has never been a time in human history well suited for the creation of knowledge, the expansion of human creativity and the enjoyment of a life of abundance like this era. There are great inventions, research, science, technology, information, communication and enterprise, all tailored to bring happiness, satisfaction, and fulfillment in the life of modern man. All these efforts, great as there are, may not have yielded the desired fruits. They have created more empty hearts and left our society more naked than ever before.

Very few individuals seem better- up in society. The sole reason is that those with great substance,position and influence are even more aggressive to acquire 'more.' This shows that their hearts are empty and they lookfor fulfillment in substance, power, position and influence- an endless search. Those who lack substance and with their minds gripped by the lack-mindset, continue to show their lack of happiness and fulfillment. We failed along the way to pass on the wisdom that happiness, satisfaction, fulfillment and joy are qualities of the mindset of abundance. We have these values only when we are in possession of this mindset.

Again, all this is because we failed along the way when we could not convince mankind that the abundance mindset is a positive, mental attitude and is the source of happiness, satisfaction and fulfillment. We also failed when we were unable to convince other fellow men, that man is wired to connect, depend on other men, exercise solidarity, cooperation and mutuality with his fellow man. We equally failed to convince mankind that happiness, satisfaction and fulfilment arequalities of the mind that is filled with abundance thoughts.Therefore, as we failed to sow and nurture these social values, negative values of greed, self-interest, jealousy and individualism grow up in their space. We find it difficult to weed.

There is fantastic accumulation of substance and wealth, packed full and overflowing in our society but most people wallow in poverty and want. This great stock of wealth cannot be shared and enjoyed by all because we lack the spiritthat generatessolidarity and the sharingand caring attitude. What we have in great quantities is jealousy, hatred, self-interest and greed. There is great abundance in our world, the inner and the outer abundance. We only need the humanizing spirit that generatessolidarity, caring,sharing and connectedness.This spirit emphasizes the fellowshipand oneness of the human family,making all abundance,the possession of all mankind.

Under this condition, all of us will enjoy the abundance of substance, wealth, power, position, influence, peace, security, a protected environment, satisfaction, happiness and fulfillment. Mark Petit in ''7 ways an abundance mindset makes your life happier and more fulfilling,'' 2019 [p. 2] submits that you can have a scarcity or an abundance mindset, that choice on which attitude to take can have a large bearing on your success. A scarcity mindset can lead to envy about what people have, guilt about what others have and anger about what other people are doing in the world. With an abundance mindset, you are more grateful, more creative and focused on collaboration.

CHAPTER FOURTEEN

ABUNDANCE IN THE FUTURE

The future holds a bright picture for abundance. This is true because technology is here with us and mankind has already experienced what technology and innovation are up to and continue to do in our society today. Technology, innovation, information communication, science, research and exploration have all created abundance in every society and defeated scarcity and lack. If some peoplestill wallow in scarcity and lack, it's not necessarily that abundance is absent, but for reasons of human greed, stinginess, jealousy, hatred and self-interest. The unprecedented leap in technological development and innovations promise to make abundance more expansive and plentiful. The intention is to make it more available and in ample supply. This abundance will only be the property of all mankind on condition that we can acquire and nurture the humanizing spirit of generosity, solidarity, interdependence, our common humanity and our desire to share. These values are generated by our abundance mindset and possess the power to open our hearts and minds sothat we can look at others as our kith and kin.

What technology and innovationshave made available to our society today will be greatly multiplied in the future. Peter Diamandis and others, in "the future is better than you think," 2013 [p. 2] make the point that humanity is now entering a period of radical transformation in which technology has the potential to significantly raise the standard of living for man, woman and child on the planet. Within a generation we will be able to provide goods and services once reserved for the wealthy few to any and all who need them. Abundance for all is really within our grasp.

But is it possible for abundance to multiply and be more abundant in future in the face of giant challenges like environmental degradation, population explosion, devastating wars, pandemics, economic and social crisis and terrorism? These appear to be gigantic impediments to human progress. Sure, these are devastating challenges to our progress but man over the years has been able to develop the capacity to go round or pierced through his wall of problems. Man has never lived in a world of no-problems and therefore through trial and error he has developed the ability to challenge his challengers.

The fact that we are still alive and kicking is proof enough that weare succeeding in the face of our challenges. It is for this reason that Peter Diamandis and others, in "abundance, summary and review," make the point that we may well think that dark times are approaching. Many of us ask ourselves: how long will it be before our world collapses under the strain of climate change, overpopulation and dwindling resources? And we answer; surely, it's just a matter of time. Abundance argues otherwise. Far from being near the end, society is on the cusp of a bright and innovative future. Changes in the world of business, technology and economics will transform societies across the globe for the better............technology and social innovation such as these will make our society a better place. Together they will help move us away from the dangers we currently face and towards a bright optimistic and abundant future.

The future of abundance will be a global issue, it will involve all mankind to think and act globally. The world must be approached as a global space made available by the creator of all mankind. There is no sense in gathering resources from Africa for the construction of Europe and America and thinking that Africa does not count. The world is for all us and life is globally interdependent and lived in cooperation and mutuality, solidarity and in the framework of abundance for all mankind. Discrimination, social exclusion and inequality are limiting values that have greatly and negatively affected our abundance. They are responsible for nursing the concepts of lack, scarcity, jealousy, greediness and hatred. Abundance cannot thrive in any environment loaded with these negative values.

We must know how to live the life of abundance in order to make abundance multiply and fill our minds and our society. Technology, innovation and information communication will produce abundance in unprecedented amounts but it won't be available to all, unless the humanizing values are present. In "what does it mean to have a life of abundance and purpose?" [p 1] the submission is made that confidence in our financial future begins with knowing how to live that abundant life that brings a real sense of meaning and purpose. In turn we become better investors as we look to what is most important to us.........we all have different gifts and abilities that we can share with our families, friends and new relationships as we look to helping others around us.........When we give of ourselves with our time and other resources to helpothers live better, we can truly say we are living the abundant life.

We cannot hesitate to praise the efforts of men and women involved inimproving the quality ofour human, physical, social and economic wellbeing. Technology, innovation and information communication together have improved the quality of human life and multiplied the stock of abundance in our societies. As the horizons of technology and innovations continue to shift, so is abundance being multiplied for humanity. There is therefore great assurance that the future of abundance is bright. Surely, mankind in future will enjoy a greater stock of abundance. But what must not be taken lightly is the fact that whether this supper abundance becomes the possession of all, will depend on society acquiring the mindset of abundance. Like I have mentioned elsewhere, the mindset of abundance is pactful with the humanizing spirit and values that universalize abundance. Without this spirit, what will be available will be consumed greedily, hoarded and individualized, bringing society back to lack, scarcity and poverty.The deciding factors remain the humanizing spirit contained in human values.

Thanks to technological innovations that despite the challenges and issues in future like wars, economic crisis and climate change, there is still hope that abundance will be created for man to live a good life. Peter Diamandis, and others, in ''abundance: the future is better than you think,'' [p 1] submitthat technologies in computing, energy, medicine and many other areas, are improving at an exponential rate and will soon enable breakthroughs that today seem impossible. These technologies have allowed independent investors to achieve startling advances in many areas of technologies with little money or manpower.

Abundance in life is nothing new. It is God's nature to supply. Abundance flows everywhere in everything. The supply of abundance to us is affected by our limiting beliefs and values. Man, from creation has the tendency to tilt his thoughtstowards scarcity, lack and want. You cannot think and believe lack, scarcity and want and expect to be filled with abundance. You can't see yourself as a poor little grasshopper and at the same time carryout the valiant activities of a giant. What the mind conceives, it brings forth same to us. How I wish we could think big, dream big, plan big and then see the giant achievements, great successes and the abundance that will manifestin our lives. Therefore, before we can hope to create our abundance, our mindset must be that of abundance. In "what does true abundance and happiness mean to you?" [P 1] the submission is made that the attainment of abundance, happiness and real wealth, begins with a conscious awareness. And it is acquired through harmonizing desire, belief and consciously focused intention and action.

It is already understood that the future will produce fantastic abundance for its people but this will come from our present planning, dreaming and envisioning. To have a bright future for abundance we must first have a vision for the future. Without a vision we will perishwithout laying hold of this abundance. The future will not drop from the sky, it has to be carefully and intelligently calculated and put together by us today. This is important so that our investment in business, information and communication, science and research will all correspond to what we want for our citizens and our society. This will ensure great abundance for our society. Mark Petit, in "7 ways an abundance mindset makes your life happier and more fulfilling," 2019 [p 4] makes the point that your vision will act like a guiding path. In your vision you can create 12 month- goals and then work back and create a specific measurable 90day goals. You can envision what your future business and life could look like as well as setting goals. You can establish the personal improvement you want to make along the way.

Abundance is the hope of all mankind. We will continue to place our hopes on the fact that our societies will grow and expand and abundance will be found everywhere. We base our hopes on the fact that as the days go by, we will graduate from lack and scarcity to the abundance mindset. We also base our hopes on the fact that we will embrace values that nurture abundance including: the humanizing spirit of solidarity, sharing, caring, generosity, interdependence, cooperation and mutuality, connectedness and the oneness of mankind. Under these conditions as mentioned above, abundance societies will be created for humanity. Without these conditions, abundance if created, will not change our miserable societies because what will be created will be hoarded, embezzled, misappropriated or egoistically consumed by the 'powerful' in society.

If our societieswill fail to nurture the above conditions which are the prerequisite to an abundance society, abundance will be a far-fetched condition for mankind.This will be true even with the highest levels attained in science, technology and innovations. But truly, there exists the opportunity for the attraction of abundance in our society as we progressively understand the law of attraction as Yap May Ling [p. 39] offers that the law of attraction is the ability to attract into our lives whatever we focus on. The law of attraction uses the power of the mind to translate whatever is in our thoughts and materializes them into reality. All thoughts turn into things, eventually.

References

- Jeff Foster, The deeper meaning of abundance [p. 2]
- Derek O' Neill, what is abundance really? [p 1]
- Leanne, is abundance about undeserved blessing? [p 1]
- Tamara Carleton, a measure of abundance [p 1]
- Martin Luther King, the philosophy of abundance [p 3]
- Remez Sasson, what is abundance, definition and explanation [p 3]
- The five traits of an abundance mindset [p 2]
- Bobby Albert, 3 traits that reflect an abundance mindset [4]
- Jim, 10 characteristics that of abundant life [p 4]
- Torsten Caspa,discover the key traits of abundance mindset [p 2]
- Ruth Soukup, living well and spending less [p 44]
- Jonathan Fields, how to live the good life [p 19]
- The Holy Bible, Galatians 5,22.
- Jivita Jay, 5 basic principles of attracting abundance and prosperity in life [p 5]
- Patrick Alley, natural resource abundance [p 3]
- Wikipedia, resource curse [p 1]
- Erwin H Bulte, resource abundance, poverty and development [p 3]
- "Old story, the risks are real.
- Success staff, 11 ways to attract abundance in your life [p 3]
- Bobbi Anderson, effortlessly attract abundance [p 1]
- Attract prosperity and abundance, living dreams [p 2]
- David Brooks, why the USA will always be rich, 2002 [p 6]

- Noctis Enoch, the greatest secret of life and reality revealed [p 1]
- What does living in abundance mean? 2020 [p 3]
- Terri Maxwell, abundance, building the life you want [p 2]
- Nicolette Stinson, 10 steps to develop an abundance mindset, 2019 [p 1]
- Jessica DW, how to shift from a scarcity to an abundance mindset, 2020 [p 3]
- Caroline Castrillon, 5 ways to go from a scarcity to an abundance mindset 2020 [p 4]
- Jo Ettle, happiness the key to abundance, 10 happiness tips.
- Jarred Buch, Uncertain futures and the importance of an abundance mindset [p 2]
- Liz Windisch, why is adopting an abundance mindset important? [p 6]
- Ben G. Yacobi, life and the pursuit of happiness 2015 [p 85]
- Mark Petit, 7 ways an abundance life makes your life happier and more fulfilling,2019 [p3]
- What does true abundance and happiness mean to you [p 7]
- Lori Keleher, authentic development, 2020 [p 2]
- Annabel Shilson-Thomas, authentic human development [p 2]
- Encyclopedia of world problems, improving the quality of human life [p 1]
- Creating abundance in a situation of poverty [p 6]
- David Martins, the purpose of abundance [p 1]
- Meg McCracken, 5 ways to discover purpose and abundance in a world that has forgotten [p3]
- The importance of an abundance mindset [p 3]

REFERENCES

- Penny Tremblay, abundance versus scarcity mindset,2017 [p 1]
- Discover the power of thought in creating abundance and happiness [p 5]
- The Holy Bible, Jerimiah 29,11
- Peter Diamandis, the future is better than what you think 2013 [p 2]
- What does it mean to have a life of abundance and purpose? [P 1]
- Yap May LING, 365 days of winning attitudes, 2017 [p.39]

www.ingramcontent.com/pod-product-compliance
Lightning Source LLC
Chambersburg PA
CBHW061432160726
47995CB00003B/855